D0677601

*f*ive Practices
of Fruitful Living

LEADER GUIDE

Robert Schnase

with

Sally D. Sharpe

ABINGDON PRESS
Nashville

Five Practices of Fruitful Living
Leader Guide

Copyright © 2010 by Abingdon Press

All rights reserved.

No part of this work may be reproduced or transmitted in any form or by any means, electronic or mechanical, including photocopying and recording, or by any information storage or retrieval system, except as may be expressly permitted by the 1976 Copyright Act or in writing from the publisher. Requests for permission can be addressed to Abingdon Press, P.O. Box 801, 201 Eighth Avenue South, Nashville, TN 37202-0801, or e-mailed to permissions@abingdonpress.com.

This book is printed on acid-free paper.

ISBN 978-1-426-71218-0

All Scripture quotations unless noted otherwise are taken from the New Revised Standard Version of the Bible, copyright 1989, Division of Christian Education of the National Council of the Churches of Christ in the United States of America. Used by permission. All rights reserved.

Scripture quotations noted (*The Message*) are from *THE MESSAGE*. Copyright © by Eugene H. Peterson 1993, 1994, 1995, 1996, 2000, 2001, 2002. Used by permission of NavPress Publishing Group.

10 11 12 13 14 15 16 17 18 19—10 9 8 7 6 5 4 3 2 1

MANUFACTURED IN THE UNITED STATES OF AMERICA

Contents

How to Use This Leader Guide

Five Practices of Fruitful Living explores how the faithful, God-related life develops with intentional and repeated attention to five practices of discipleship that are critical for our growth in Christ:

1. Radical Hospitality
2. Passionate Worship
3. Intentional Faith Development
4. Risk-Taking Mission and Service
5. Extravagant Generosity

This Leader Guide is designed to walk groups through an experientially-based study of these Five Practices, with the expected results of growth in Christ, a deepening of the spiritual life, a greater capacity to live fruitfully and fully, and the desire and ability to become instruments of God's transforming grace. Your group will discover that ongoing attention to these Five Practices will open their hearts to God, to others, and to a life that matters—a life rich with meaning, relationship, and contribution.

Because this study is personal and practical in both subject matter and approach, you will find it appropriate for a wide variety of groups and settings, including Sunday school classes, discipleship and study groups, house groups, committees and teams, new member classes, weekend retreats, and more.

This study material is rich, personal, and focuses on a lifetime journey rather than short-term solutions. Ideally, you may want class sessions of 90 minutes or more for full group discussion. Many groups depend on the Sunday morning setting, so within the body of this guide, you'll find session plans for six weekly sessions of 45–60 minutes each, plus an optional orientation session. If using the shorter class settings, you may want to reference the appendix model for studying each book chapter in two sessions. Another option, if you are using a shorter class session, is to encourage class members to covenant with one another for conversations outside the class time, discussing their experiences to stay engaged and deepen the study experience. Whether 45 minutes or 2 hours, the time your group spends studying the Five Practices can be transformative as you learn to cultivate a fruitful life in God.

In addition to models for a 90-minute group session, a 12-week study, and a weekend retreat, in the appendix you will find optional activities and ideas for other uses. For example, small groups throughout the church might study the material simultaneously for a church-wide emphasis during Lent or another designated time. However you choose to use it, the key to a successful study is to make it your own. Feel free to adapt, modify, or expand the materials and ideas in this guide as you wish to meet the specific needs of your group/church.

A Quick Overview of the Group Session

Each session outline has four segments: 1) Getting Ready, 2) Getting Started, 3) Digging In, and 4) Making Application.

1. Getting Ready

This segment of the session outline provides material for your preparation as leader, including a key Scripture, a summary of main ideas from the corresponding chapter in *Five Practices of Fruitful Living*, and 3–5 focus points selected from the main ideas. Note that the material in the segment *Digging In* pertains only to these focus points. If you would like to select other focus points from the main ideas, either as substitutes or as additions for an extended session, simply identify supporting material in the chapter and create several appropriate discussion starters or questions for each.

Before each group session, read the corresponding chapter in *Five Practices of Fruitful Living* and notify participants to be reading the chapter as well. Familiarize yourself with the session outline, select the leader cues and discussion questions you will include, write the key Scripture and focus points on a chart or board, and pray for the session and group members.

2. Getting Started

This segment of the outline actually opens the session. During this time you will welcome participants and offer a prayer. Feel free to use the prayer provided or to say your own prayer. Following the prayer, direct participants' attention to the key

Scripture and focus points written on the board/chart. You may read them aloud or have a group member do so. Consider having several group members read the key Scripture from several different Bible translations.

3. Digging In

Given the personal nature of the study, this segment of the group session is designed to be more fluid than segmented so that participants engage in discussion and share stories as they consider each point. This approach acknowledges that the faith journey is experiential rather than systematic or dogmatic. You will guide participants through this process by reading or following leader cues and facilitating group discussion after each. To stay on schedule for a 45–60-minute session, you will need to pick and choose from the material provided. Determine in advance which leader cues and discussion questions you will include and put a checkmark beside them.

Each leader cue instructs participants to recall and/or locate material from the corresponding chapter in *Five Practices of Fruitful Living*, which they were to read prior to the group session. Because some participants may not have read the chapter, it will be helpful to pause momentarily so that everyone may locate and briefly scan the material. As you move into group discussion, encourage participants to share even if they are seeing the material for the first time. The faith journey is deeply personal, and real growth occurs as we engage in honest reflection and conversation about our experiences, hopes, and questions.

4. Making Application

The final segment of the group session focuses on the application of the given practice in everyday life. During this time participants will consider three questions:

What Does It Look Like? *What is this practice and how does it appear in daily life?*
What Are the Obstacles? *What are the barriers to living this way?*
What Now? *How can I practice this in my life—today? This year? For a lifetime?*

As participants hear the stories of real people living out a given practice, they will find glimpses of themselves, clues to their own callings, and encouragement for pursuing the practice in their own lives. During this time they also will identify and address some of the obstacles to implementing the practice, as well as consider what they are going to do differently in the coming weeks, months, and years.

Helpful Hints

As you prepare to lead your group and facilitate group discussion, here are a few helpful hints to keep in mind:

- Read the corresponding chapter in *Five Practice of Fruitful Living* and review the session outline prior to the group session.
- Determine whether you will focus on the suggested focus points or substitute others. Remember that you will need to create your own leader cues and discussion questions for these points.
- Cultivate an atmosphere of hospitality at every step of the process of inviting, hosting, and welcoming people to each session with attention to the meeting space, seating, time, childcare, refreshments, and attitude of mutual care. Pray for one another and help people feel welcome, accepted, encouraged, and supported in their spiritual exploration.
- Communicate the experiential nature of the study and the benefit of honest and open conversation—for them as individuals and as a community of faith. Encourage individuals to share their own stories and experiences as they are willing.
- If no one responds at first, do not be afraid of a little silence. Count to seven silently; then say something such as, "Would anyone like to go first?" If everyone remains silent, venture a response yourself. Then ask for comments and other responses.
- Model openness as you share with the group. Group members will follow your example. If you share at a surface level, everyone else will follow suit.

- Draw out participants without asking them to share what they are unwilling to share. Make eye contact with someone and say something such as, "How about someone else?"
- Encourage multiple responses before moving on.
- Ask "Why?" or "Why do you believe that?" to help continue a discussion and give it greater depth.
- Affirm others' responses with comments such as, "Great" or "Thanks" or "Good insight"—especially if this is the first time someone has spoken during the session.
- Give everyone a chance to talk, but keep the conversation moving. Moderate to prevent a few individuals from doing all the talking.
- Monitor your own contributions. If you are doing most of the talking, back off so that you do not train the group not to respond.
- Remember that you do not have to have all the "answers." Your job is to keep the discussion going and encourage participation.
- Honor the time schedule. If a session is running longer than expected, get consensus from the group before continuing beyond the agreed-upon ending time.

Finally and most importantly, remember to pray. Pray for God to prepare and equip you, pray for your group members individually, and pray for God's presence and leading before each session. More than anything else, prayer will encourage and empower you for the weeks ahead.

May your group experience result in greater fruitfulness in Christ—both for you and for your group members.

Orientation Session

(45–50 minutes)

1. Getting Ready
(Prior to the Session)

Preparation
- Announce the orientation session in the church bulletin, newsletter, and/or website. (Optional: Distribute copies of *Five Practices of Fruitful Living* prior to the session with instructions to read the introduction prior to the orientation session.)
- Read the introduction in *Five Practices of Fruitful Living*, as well as the "How to Use" section of this Leader Guide.
- Review the orientation session outline.
- Write the key Scripture and focus points on a board or chart.
- Write the dates and times for future group sessions on a board or chart, or prepare a handout with this information.
- Prepare the meeting space to maximize a sense of welcome and hospitality, with attention to signs, greeters, seating, name tags, or refreshments.
- Pray for the session and for those who will be attending.

Key Scripture
"I am the vine, you are the branches. Those who abide in me and I in them bear much fruit. . . . My father is glorified by this, that you bear much fruit and become my disciples." —John 15:5, 8

Summary of Main Ideas:
Introduction, *Five Practices of Fruitful Living*
- The fruitful, God-related life develops with intentional and repeated attention to five essential practices that are critical for our growth in Christ: Radical Hospitality, Passionate Worship, Intentional Faith Development, Risk-Taking Mission and Service, and Extravagant Generosity.
- The Five Practices are rooted in Scripture and derived from the clear imperatives of the life of Christ.

11

- This study is based on the premise that by repeating and deepening certain fundamental practices, we cooperate with God in our own growth in Christ and participate with the Holy Spirit in our own spiritual maturation.
- Through the Five Practices, we open ourselves to grace and let ourselves be opened by grace. As a result, we are changed; we become new creations in Christ.
- Every step of the journey toward Christ is preceded by, made possible by, and sustained by the perfecting grace of God. However, becoming the persons God desires us to become is also the fruit of a persistent, deeply personal, and active quest.
- This study will be most successful if the leader and participants agree to . . .
  - approach the conversation/discussion with honesty and openness;
  - share their personal experiences, recognizing that none of us has the complete picture;
  - focus on practical application that is more like a compass than a map (helpful direction without a step-by-step plan);
  - engage the material personally, discovering what they can learn about themselves, their relationship with God, their personal desires, and their resistances in the life of faith;
  - and commit to carefully read the corresponding chapter in *Five Practices of Fruitful Living* prior to each group session, leaving time to consider the questions for reflection at the end of each chapter.

 ## Focus Points

1. The fruitful, God-related life develops with intentional and repeated attention to five essential practices that are critical for our growth in Christ: Radical Hospitality, Passionate Worship, Intentional Faith Development, Risk-Taking Mission and Service, and Extravagant Generosity.
2. Through persistent repetition of the Five Practices, we grow in Christ and cooperate with the Holy Spirit in our spiritual maturation. As a result, we are changed—we become new creations in Christ.

3. God's grace makes every step of the journey possible, yet our persistent and active quest is vitally important.
4. This study will be most successful if participants commit to...
    - share openly and honestly;
    - focus on practical application (helpful direction without a step-by-step plan);
    - engage the material personally;
    - and read the corresponding chapter in *Five Practices of Fruitful Living* prior to each session.

2. Getting Started
(5 minutes)

Welcome and Overview

After a brief welcome, distribute copies of *Five Practices of Fruitful Living* if you did not do so prior to the session. Explain that this orientation session will roughly follow the basic outline of the group sessions in the study. (Note, however, that the suggested times for the segments in this orientation session differ slightly from those in the weekly 60-minute group sessions.) The intent is two-fold: to give a sense of the format and flow of a typical session, and to provide a foundation of understanding regarding the purpose and intent of the study.

Briefly present the format of the group sessions:

Welcome
Opening Prayer
Key Scripture / Focus Points (*Focal Scripture and Main Points of the Session*)
Leader Cues / Group Discussion (*Leader Helps and Group Discussion Questions*)
What Does It Look Like? (*Practical Help/Encouragement for Pursuing the Practice*)
What Are the Obstacles? (*Resistances or Challenges to Implementing the Practice*)
What Now? (*Personal Commitment to Application*)

Opening Prayer

Gracious God, you have invited us into a relationship with you that is vibrant, dynamic, and fruitful. Jesus said that he is the vine and we are the branches, and that if we abide in him and he in us, we bear much fruit. This is your desire for us—that we walk closely with Jesus and bear much fruit as his disciples. And so we are gathered here today to learn more about how to have an abundant, purposeful, deep, and fruitful life in and through Jesus Christ. Teach us the practices that will open us to your grace so that we may be changed and become agents of change in the world for your purposes. Amen.

Scripture / Focus Points

Direct participants' attention to the key Scripture and focus points for this orientation session. You may read them aloud, or have a group member do so, if you choose.

3. Digging In
(30–40 minutes)

 ## Focus Point #1:

The fruitful, God-related life develops with intentional and repeated attention to five essential practices that are critical for our growth in Christ: Radical Hospitality, Passionate Worship, Intentional Faith Development, Risk-Taking Mission and Service, and Extravagant Generosity.

Leader Cue

Have participants turn to p. 8 in *Five Practices of Fruitful Living*. Briefly review the Five Practices and note that the failure to attend to, develop, and deepen these practices with intentionality limits our capacity to live fruitfully and fully.

Read aloud the following excerpt from p. 9: *"These practices open our heart—to God, to others, to a life that matters, a life rich with meaning, relationship, and contribution. They help us flourish."*

Group Discussion
- Why do you think the Five Practices are essential to growth in Christ and to the deepening of the spiritual life?
- Share how one of the Five Practices has helped you to flourish in some way in your own spiritual life.

 FOCUS POINT #2:

Through persistent repetition of the Five Practices, we grow in Christ and cooperate with the Holy Spirit in our spiritual maturation. As a result, we are changed—we become new creations in Christ.

Leader Cue

Present several of the analogies of the effects of persistent and repetitious practice found on pp. 10–11.

Group Discussion
- How has persistent repetition of Christian practices changed you over time?

 FOCUS POINT #3:

God's grace makes every step of the journey possible, yet our persistent and active quest is vitally important.

Leader Cue

Direct participants' attention to pp. 11–12. Read aloud the following excerpt:

"The Christian life is a gift of God, an expression of God's grace in Christ, the result of an undeserved and unmerited offering of love toward us. . . . However, becoming the person that God desires us to become is also the fruit of a persistent and deeply personal quest. . . . The fruitful life is cultivated by placing ourselves in the most advantageous places to see, receive, learn, and understand the love that has been offered in Christ."

Point out that the practices of early Christians included worshiping, learning Scripture, serving one another, and sharing generously.

Note that early Wesleyans were chided as "Methodists" because of the nearly eccentric adherence to methodical ways of systemizing the practices of the Christian faith to promote learning, service, and growth in Christ through daily and weekly exercises and patterns. Personal practices included worship, singing, fasting, and receiving the sacraments; searching Scripture and participating in classes and covenant groups for spiritual encouragement and accountability; serving the poor and visiting the sick and imprisoned; and tithing their incomes.

Group Discussion
- How has God's grace played a part in the change that has occurred thus far in your Christian journey?
- What part have you played in bringing about this change and cultivating fruitfulness in your life?
- What specific practices of the Christian faith do you find most meaningful or satisfying?

 FOCUS POINT #4:

This study will be most successful if participants commit to...

- **share openly and honestly;**
- **focus on practical application (helpful direction without a step-by-step plan);**
- **engage the material personally;**
- **and read the corresponding chapter in *Five Practices of Fruitful Living* prior to each session.**

Leader Cue
Read each statement aloud one at a time, followed by an excerpt from *Five Practices of Fruitful Living*.

1) As we engage in group discussion, you are encouraged to share openly and honestly.

"Henri Nouwen believed that what is personal is most universal. When we think we may be the only person who has ever felt a certain way, doubted or feared or resisted in a certain manner, we discover that such experience is usually what we have most in common with others in their

innermost lives. . . . In other people, we find glimpses of ourselves; in their shortfalls, we see our own more clearly; in their callings, we find clues to our own. . . . [This study] relies on the experiences of ordinary people who have been extraordinarily shaped by their relationship to God. None of us has the complete picture." (pp. 13–14)

2) This study is practical.

"It is about what we do daily and intentionally, and about who we become because of how God uses what we do. It suggests a compass rather than a map; a direction helpful for many diverse contexts rather than a specific step-by-step, how-to plan that fits only certain terrain." (p. 14)

3) If you will engage the material personally, you will experience significant benefits.

"Discover what you can learn about yourself, your relationship with God, your personal desires and internal resistances in the life of faith." (p. 14)

4) You are encouraged to read one chapter in *Five Practices for Fruitful Living* prior to each group session.

"This book is about how we learn from [others'] fruitfulness in Christ so that we cooperate with God in becoming what God created us to be. My prayer for you and [the group] is that Five Practices for Fruitful Living *helps us all grow in grace and in the knowledge and love of God. May we be changed from the inside out so that we can transform the world for the purposes of Christ."* (p. 15)

Group Discussion
- When was a time you discovered that the more fully you participate in a study, the more you get from it?

4. Making Application
(5–10 minutes)

What Does It Look Like?
Explain that during this segment of the group session, you will explore examples and habits of people who live out the given practice.

Ask:
  • Why are stories and examples helpful when it comes to making personal application?

What Are the Obstacles?
Explain that during this time the group will explore some of the more common obstacles—resistances and challenges—to implementing the given practice, as we discuss which obstacle or obstacles are most challenging to you personally.

What Now?
Explain that at the conclusion of each group session, participants will be instructed to reflect silently in response to this question:

  • In light of all we have shared today, what do you sense God saying to you?

Invite participants to reflect on this question now. (Allow 15–20 seconds for reflection.)

Tell group members that after reflecting on this, they will be invited to share "popcorn" answers to the questions: "In response, what will you do differently this week?" and "How will what you learned this week change how you live your life?" (*Popcorn* refers to quick, spontaneous comments from class members. Sometimes the leader will have to wait a minute before the "corn" begins to pop, but when the group warms up, people will offer their insights and thoughts.) Explain that for this orientation session, they are simply invited to continue reflecting on all they have heard today.

Conclude by inviting participants to sign up for the study. In advance, create a sign-up sheet with spaces for name, address, phone, and e-mail. Be prepared to address any questions that may arise about childcare, meeting times and places, parking, or other practical matters. Direct their attention to the meeting dates and times, or distribute the information handout at this time.

Receiving God's Love

The Practice of Radical Hospitality

1. Getting Ready
(Prior to the Session)

Preparation
- Read Chapter 1 in *Five Practices of Fruitful Living*.
- Write the key Scripture and focus points on a board or chart.
- Review *Digging In* and *Making Application*, and select the leader cues and discussion questions you will cover.
- Pray for the session and for your group members.

Key Scripture
"We love because he first loved us." —1 John 4:19

Summary of Main Ideas: Chapter 1
- The first step in our walk of faith is saying *Yes* to God's unconditional love for us. In the words of Paul Tillich, we accept that we are accepted, and in that moment we are "struck by grace"[1]—we receive the love and forgiveness of God, begin to comprehend its meaning, and open ourselves to the new life it brings.
- Radical Hospitality involves being receptive to God's love and intentionally making room for God in our lives. It is the key to all the practices that lead to fruitful living.
- Grace is the active, reaching, gift-like quality of God's love. God's grace seeks us and unexpectedly breaks open our hearts, changing us and working its way through us to others.
- Jesus is the ultimate expression of God's grace.

- Faith is our acceptance of God's gift of grace. We receive God's grace, love, and pardon, and allow these gifts to shape us and make us anew.
- There are many obstacles that prevent us from receiving God's love and make us inhospitable to God's initiative; including cultural voices; fast-forward living; negative internal messages; and our own attitudes, choices, and behaviors.
- The good life comes from opening ourselves to God's grace, and often we come to a place of receptivity through unexpected moments or events.

 ## FOCUS POINTS

1. Radical Hospitality involves being receptive to God's love and intentionally making room for God in our lives.
2. Grace is the initiating, gift-like quality of God's love that seeks us and changes us. Jesus is the ultimate expression of God's grace.
3. Faith is our acceptance of God's gift of grace.
4. The good life comes from patterns of opening ourselves to God's grace rather than closing ourselves off from God—from saying *Yes* to the spiritual life rather than *No*—and often we come to a place of receptivity through unexpected moments or events.

2. Getting Started
(5 minutes)

Welcome

Opening Prayer

Gracious God, you love us unconditionally and accept us unreservedly. Because of your great love for us, you pursue us and break into our lives with the gift of your amazing grace, offering us forgiveness, restoration, wholeness, and abundant life through your Son, Jesus—the ultimate expression of your grace. All we have to do is open ourselves to your love and accept your gift. It is so simple, and yet there arc so many voices and distractions that threaten to keep us from being receptive to your love. Help us to overcome these obstacles and to become more receptive to you. Teach us to cultivate the practice of Radical Hospitality in our lives, of opening ourselves again and again to you and making a place in our hearts for your love. In Jesus' name we pray. Amen.

Scripture / Focus Points

Direct participants' attention to the key Scripture and focus points. You may read them aloud, or have a group member do so, if you choose.

3. Digging In
(25–30 minutes)

Note: More material is provided than you will be able to cover in 25–30 minutes. In advance of the session, select the leader cues and discussion questions you will include and put a checkmark beside them.

 ## FOCUS POINT #1:

Radical Hospitality involves being receptive to God's love and intentionally making room for God in our lives.

Leader Cue

Direct participants to p. 17 in *Five Practices of Fruitful Living*. Have someone read the first paragraph aloud.

Now have participants turn to p. 18. Read aloud the following passage (middle of the page), emphasizing the underlined words and pausing as indicated:

"You are <u>loved</u>. [pause] You <u>are</u> loved. [pause] <u>You</u> are loved. [pause] "Can you accept that?
"God's love for us is not something we have to strive for, earn, work on, or fear. It is freely given. That is key: that we are loved, first, finally, and forever by God, a love so deep and profound and significant that God offers his Son to signify and solidify this love forever so that we get it."

Group Discussion

- How have you felt/experienced God's unconditional love?
- Have you truly accepted that you are loved and accepted by God? If not, what is keeping you from accepting this reality?
- Have you ever felt that you must strive for, earn, or fear God's love? Why?

Leader Cue

Direct participants back to p. 17. Briefly present Tillich's concept of being "struck by grace." Emphasize the following points:

- When God's grace strikes us, we are faced with the startling reality of God's unconditional love for us.
- This realization jars us into a new way of thinking.
- Receiving and understanding the love and forgiveness of God opens us to new life, and this can be as abrupt as lightening and as disruptive as an earthquake.

Group Discussion

- What do you understand the phrase "struck by grace" to mean?
- How have you been struck by God's grace?

Leader Cue

Have participants turn to p. 19. Ask someone to read aloud "Just Say Yes!" found at the bottom of the page.

Group Discussion

- When have you said *Yes* to God when you could have said *No*, and what difference has this made for you?

 FOCUS POINT #2:

Grace is the initiating, gift-like quality of God's love that seeks us and changes us. Jesus is the ultimate expression of God's grace.

Leader Cue

Have someone read aloud the key Scripture: 1 John 4:19 (perhaps from a different translation this time), followed by Ephesians 2:8.

Next, read aloud the following excerpt from the bottom of p. 21: *"It's not that we love first, but that we are first loved. This active, reaching quality of God's love is what* grace *refers to, a gift-like initiative on God's part toward us."*

Group Discussion

- Through what persons, experiences, or events have you encountered the initiating, gift-like quality of God's grace?
- How have you been changed by God's grace?

Leader Cue

Direct participants to p. 23. Read aloud the following excerpts:

"Jesus is the ultimate expression of God's grace, God becoming human in order to reach us and to make possible living abundantly, meaningfully, lovingly, and gracefully."

"The God we see revealed in Jesus is the God of grace, *an active, searching, embracing, assertive love."*

Highlight some of the descriptions of God's grace as demonstrated through Jesus:

- *strong, persevering, gritty grace*—that embraced untouchables and outcasts
- *courageous grace*—that interceded against violence and injustice on behalf of a woman accused of adultery
- *earthy, practical grace*—that modeled servanthood by washing the disciples' feet
- *unrelenting, irresistible grace*—that never gave up on the hopeless or the powerful
- *disturbing, interruptive grace*—that overturned the tables of the money changers in the Temple
- *perceptive, affirming grace*—that noticed a widow with her two coins and a mourning father
- *compassionate grace*—that embraced victims of violence
- *persistent grace*—that stepped into cell blocks with prisoners

> - *challenging, correcting, indicting grace*—that confronted unsympathetic rich people and haughty religious leaders
> - *costly, sacrificial grace*—that absorbed the violence of humiliation, unjust persecution, and torturous death to reveal the depth of God's love for humanity

Group Discussion

- How have you seen the active, searching, unrelenting grace of God at work to reach someone with God's love?
- How have you experienced the grace of God through Jesus? How would you describe this grace?

 ## FOCUS POINT #3:

Faith is our acceptance of God's gift of grace.

Leader Cue

Have someone reread Ephesians 2:8 aloud for the group.

Point out that the apostle Paul said there are two essential and operative elements to a whole and right relationship with God: *grace* and *faith*. Remind participants of the gift analogy found at the bottom of p. 22. Grace is God's gift to us. Faith is our acceptance of God's gift.

Read aloud the following excerpt from the bottom of p. 22: "Faith *is our acceptance of the gift, the opening of our hearts to invite God's love into our lives.* Faith *is our receiving God's grace, love, and pardon, and allowing these gifts to shape us and make us anew.* Faith *is the commitment again and again to live by grace, to honor the gift, and use it, and pass it along.*"

Group Discussion

- Why are both grace and faith necessary for a right, whole relationship with God?
- What part has faith played in your practice of Radical Hospitality—your ability to say *Yes* to God and make room for God in your life?

Focus Point #4:

The good life comes from patterns of opening ourselves to God's grace rather than closing ourselves off from God—from saying *Yes* to the spiritual life rather than *No*—and often we come to a place of receptivity through unexpected moments or events.

Leader Cue

Direct participants to p. 33. Read aloud the following excerpt:

"We never earn enough, do enough, or achieve enough to guarantee happiness. We do not become what God created us to be simply by more activity, faster motion, working harder, or having more stuff. . . . And contrary to self-help books, the good life cannot come from inside us or by our own efforts either. We do not achieve it by trying harder, pushing further, pulling ourselves up by our own bootstraps. . . . The good life comes from the practice of hospitality toward God, opening ourselves to God, and making room in our hearts for the gift-like transformation God's love makes possible."

Briefly review the things mentioned at the bottom of the page that result in the happiness found in "the good life":
- patterns of living that draw us closer to God
- practices that open and reopen the connections that bind us to God and the community
- learning to love and be loved
- serving and being served
- focusing outward, offering ourselves to make a difference

Group Discussion
- Compare the inner happiness that comes from God's Spirit with the happiness defined by culture.
- What personal patterns and practices help you to cultivate the good life?

> ## Leader Cue
> Point out that sometimes we are not receptive to God's grace until unexpected situations or experiences break into our interior lives, causing us to ask questions and making us aware of our yearning.

Group Discussion
- What unexpected moments or situations have brought you to a new or deeper receptivity to God and God's grace?

4. Making Application
(15–20 minutes)

What Does It Look Like?
Have participants turn to Mitch's story, beginning on p. 34. Be prepared to summarize the story, noting the highlights.

Briefly discuss:
- What signs of receptivity can you identify in Mitch's story— moments when he could have said *No* but instead said *Yes* to God?

Direct participants to the section "Practicing Radical Hospitality Toward God," beginning on p. 36. Point out that Radical Hospitality involves receptivity and intentional practice. Then highlight the habits of people who practice Radical Hospitality.

People who practice Radical Hospitality . . .
- Look for ways to invite God in.
- Deliberately say *Yes* to promptings of the Spirit.
- Regularly ask for God's help.
- Desire God's presence.
- Make space in their lives and hearts for "soul work."
- Welcome interruptions by God into their lives and see them as opportunities.
- Look for evidence of God's presence and work.
- Seek to know God more and learn new things.
- Allow God to become the fundamental and defining part of their life.

- Practice, repeat, and deepen the core essentials that open themselves to God.
- Say *No* to other things so that they may say *Yes* to God.
- Open themselves to the community of faith.
- Are willing to wrestle with God.
- Are validated by God's love and acceptance.
- Seek first God's kingdom.

Ask:
- How do your present patterns of living invite God in or cause you to avoid the spiritual life?

What Are the Obstacles?

Acknowledge that there are many obstacles that prevent us from receiving God's love and make us inhospitable to God's initiative (see pp. 25–32). Highlight the four categories outlined in the book:

- Cultural voices (television, radio, magazines, billboards, the Internet, iPods, cell phones, etc.)
- Fast-forward living (high-tech and highly mobile lifestyles)
- Negative internal messages (negative voices of family members or other influential persons in our lives)
- Our own attitudes, choices, and behaviors (selfishness, self-preoccupation, self-absorption, destructive decisions and habits)

Briefly discuss:
- Which obstacles or distractions keep you from fully receiving God's love?

What Now?

Instruct participants to reflect silently in response to this question:

- In light of all we have shared today, what do you sense God saying to you?

(Allow 15–20 seconds for reflection.)

End by inviting each participant to share short, "popcorn" answers to these questions:

- In response, what will you do differently this week?
- How will what you learned this week change how you live your life?

As participants prepare to leave, ask them to take time in the coming days to journal or silently meditate on the following questions. You may wish to write these on a board or chart or slips of paper to hand out to each participant. Invite them to share their thoughts or ideas with a prayer partner, family member, friend, or classmate as they are comfortable:

- What would greater receptivity or openness to God look like for my life?
- Thinking about the next 3–5 years, what patterns do I hope God will use to reshape my life? How will I begin these patterns/practices?

Loving God in Return

The Practice of Passionate Worship

1. Getting Ready
(Prior to the Session)

Preparation
- Read Chapter 2 in *Five Practices of Fruitful Living*.
- Write the key Scripture and focus points on a board or chart.
- Review *Digging In* and *Making Application*, and select the leader cues and discussion questions you will cover.
- Pray for the session and for your group members.

Key Scripture
"You shall love the Lord your God with all your heart, and with all your soul, and with all your strength, and with all your mind; and your neighbor as yourself." —Luke 10:27

Summary of Main Ideas: Chapter 2
- Worship expresses our love for God in response to God's great love for us.
- Worship changes us. It is a means of grace, a way for God to accomplish our re-creation.
- Worship . . .
  - connects us to God and to others who love God.
  - helps us to discover the transcendent, spiritual aspects of life.
  - puts us in the most advantageous place for engaging the Spirit and focusing on God.

- brings us back to ourselves, grounding us in what really matters.
- Passionate Worship is a dynamic, vibrant expression of a fruitful relationship with God—not a routine or performance-driven experience.
- There is great mystery in worship. Somehow visible and tangible rituals and actions result in us feeling sustained, grounded, forgiven, connected, motivated to make better choices, and called to serve.
- Daily personal prayer and worship deepen our relationship with God and prepare us for community worship.
- Passionate Worship requires us to surrender or relinquish ourselves and our will—including all external and internal resistances to worship.
- The practice of Passionate Worship becomes a valued and sustaining pattern that affects every aspect of one's life.

 ## FOCUS POINTS

1. Worship expresses our love for God and connects us to God.
2. Worship changes us; it is a means of grace.
3. There is great mystery in worship.
4. Passionate Worship is a dynamic, vibrant expression of a fruitful relationship with God.

2. Getting Started
(5 minutes)

Welcome

Opening Prayer
Loving God, we are so thankful for your unconditional and unending love for us. Your love is so amazing that we want to respond by loving and adoring you in return. We long to draw close to you and connect with you in worship, and we know that when we do, we are changed. Help us to make worship a priority

in our lives, and teach us to be passionate worshipers. In Jesus' name we pray. Amen.

Scripture / Focus Points

Direct participants' attention to the key Scripture and focus points. You may read them aloud, or have a group member do so, if you choose.

3. Digging In
(25–30 minutes)

Note: More material is provided than you will be able to cover in 25–30 minutes. In advance of the session, select the leader cues and discussion questions you will include and put a checkmark beside them.

 ## FOCUS POINT #1:

Worship expresses our love for God and connects us to God.

Leader Cue

Ask someone to read aloud 1 John 4:19, which was the key Scripture for Session 1.

Direct participants to the paragraph under the heading "Worship" on p. 45 in *Five Practices of Fruitful Living*. (Pause briefly, giving them time to scan the paragraph.) Draw special attention to this sentence: *"We love God in return."*

Group Discussion
- Why is it helpful to understand that worship is a *response* to God's love?
- How does your awareness of God's love for you fuel your worship?

Leader Cue

Direct participants to turn to p. 47. Have someone read aloud the last sentence in the first paragraph: *"God desires a relationship with us, and in response to God's seeking us, worship is our way of seeking God, our reaching upward to God's reaching downward."*

Group Discussion
- What are some ways we "reach upward to God" in worship?
- Describe a time when you felt connected to God in worship.

Leader Cue

Have someone reread the key Scripture: Luke 10:27 (perhaps from a different translation this time).

Then read aloud this sentence from the middle of p. 46: *"Heart, mind, soul, and strength—in worship we offer all to God in love."*

Group Discussion
- What does it look like to offer all—heart, mind, soul, and strength—to God in love through worship?

 ## FOCUS POINT #2:

Worship changes us; it is a means of grace.

Leader Cue

Direct participants to the paragraph that begins at the bottom of p. 45 and continues at the top of p. 46. (Pause briefly, giving them time to find the paragraph.) Have someone read the paragraph aloud.

Group Discussion
- What are some ways God changes us in worship?

- When has a worship experience changed your heart and mind and provided you with fresh spiritual insights?
- What about worship refreshes and replenishes you?

Leader Cue

Have participants turn to p. 51 and direct their attention to the paragraphs on the top half of the page. (Pause briefly, giving them time to scan the paragraphs.)

Emphasize God's activity in worship by reading aloud the following sentences: *"The purpose of worship does not begin and end with what human beings do; worship is the means God uses to accomplish God's purposes in the human heart and in the community of Christ. God is active in worship even when we are not."*

Point out the following:
- God does not desire our praise because God needs it, but because it opens our hearts to God's love and directs our hearts toward the following of God's ways.
- God desires our praise because God desires what is best for us. In worship we can confess our brokenness, receive pardon, relieve our guilt, and be redirected. It is a means of grace through which God actually re-creates us.

Group Discussion
- How do these ideas enlighten your understanding or view of worship?
- Why is it important to see worship from God's point of view, and how can this benefit us as worshipers?

Leader Cue

Briefly present the "gardener of the soul" analogy found at the end of this section (middle of p. 51).

Group Discussion
- How can the gardening analogy enrich our understanding and experience of worship?

- How have you experienced God doing some "gardening" in your heart and soul through worship? What growth and fruit have resulted?

 ## FOCUS POINT #3:

There is great mystery in worship.

Leader Cue
Direct participants to p. 53, and have someone read the first paragraph aloud.

Group Discussion
- What aspects of worship involve and express a sense of mystery? Which of these is most significant to you personally and why?

Leader Cue
Have participants turn to p. 55. Read aloud "A Converting Sacrament," or retell the story in your own words.

Group Discussion
- How did Carl experience the sacrament of Holy Communion as a means of grace? How did it change him and, ultimately, his life?
- Think of an experience of Holy Communion that particularly moved you. What made it especially meaningful?

Leader Cue
Direct participants' attention to pp. 55–57. Acknowledge that music is another element of worship involving great mystery. Somehow it shapes the human spirit. Point out some of the many ways music affects us:

- Lifts us to God
- Moves us to profound contemplation
- Opens us to the interior life (makes us receptive spiritually)
- Touches the depths of the soul
- Expresses emotions and ideas that are difficult to communicate
- Writes truths upon our hearts
- Unifies and binds us together

Group Discussion

- Why do you think music affects us so profoundly?
- How would you describe what worship would be like without music?
- Share a time when you felt your spirit moved or lifted up to God by music in worship.
- How does singing make a difference in your spiritual life?

Leader Cue

Read aloud the following excerpt from p. 57: *"Perhaps the greatest mystery involves how the affectionate attention to ordinary things in worship . . . reveals a beauty, depth, meaning, and coherence that opens us to the discovery and rediscovery of grace in everyday situations throughout the week. Worship trains our attentiveness to God, attunes us to noticing the Spirit."*

Group Discussion

- How has worship helped you to be more attuned to God throughout the week? How has it helped you to see God's work, sense God's presence, and discern God's call more naturally?

 FOCUS POINT #4:

Passionate Worship is a dynamic, vibrant expression of a fruitful relationship with God.

Leader Cue

Direct participants' attention to the section "The Practice of Passionate Worship" found on pp. 60–61. Summarize the section by presenting five "P's" of practicing Passionate Worship: 1) prioritize, 2) prepare, 3) participate, 4) pray, and 5) persist. (Write them on a board or chart, if you wish.)

People who practice Passionate Worship . . .
- Prioritize worship and shift their schedules accordingly.
- Prepare their hearts and minds for worship by praying, reading Scripture, and anticipating how God will connect to them.
- Participate by taking notes, singing from their souls, offering their services in worship, and contributing to an atmosphere of expectation.
- Pray regularly, developing a habit of prayer.
- Persist wholeheartedly in cultivating their relationship with God.

Group Discussion
- Why are all five P's necessary for Passionate Worship? What happens to an individual's worship experience when any of them is missing?
- Which of the five P's comes most easily to you and why? Which is most difficult or challenging and why?

4. Making Application
(15–20 minutes)

What Does It Look Like?

Remind participants of Helen's story, found on pp. 62–64. Be prepared to summarize the story, noting the highlights.

Briefly discuss:
- How did Helen's lifelong practice of loving and worshiping God impact her life and the lives of others?
- How does Helen's story encourage you to pursue the practice of Passionate Worship?

What Are the Obstacles?

Acknowledge that there are many obstacles or resistances to worship (see pp. 58–60), and suggest that participants focus their attention on four categories. Review each briefly:

- Awkwardness due to unfamiliarity (with people, rituals, routines, worship styles, etc.)
- Competing obligations, habits, interests
- Resistance, criticism, or ridicule of others
- Internal resistances, such as boredom, disinterest, or doubts

Briefly discuss:
- How does overcoming these obstacles involve a surrendering of ourselves and of our will?
- When have you felt discomfort or resistance to the experience of worship? How did you work through it?

What Now?

Instruct participants to reflect silently in response to this question:

- In light of all we have shared today, what do you sense God saying to you?

(Allow 15–20 seconds for reflection.)

End by inviting each participant to share short, "popcorn" answers to these questions:

- In response, what will you do differently this week?
- How will what you learned this week change how you live your life?

As participants prepare to leave, ask them to take time in the coming days to journal or silently meditate on the following questions. You may wish to write these on a board or chart or slips of paper to hand out to each participant. Invite them to share their thoughts or ideas with a prayer partner, family member, friend, or classmate as they are comfortable:

- What does a passionate worship experience look like for my life?
- Thinking about the next 3–5 years, what patterns do I hope God will use to reshape my life? How will I begin these patterns/practices?

Growing in Grace

The Practice of Intentional Faith Development

1. Getting Ready
(Prior to the Session)

Preparation
- Read Chapter 3 in *Five Practices of Fruitful Living*.
- Write the key Scripture and focus points on a board or chart.
- Review *Digging In* and *Making Application*, and select the leader cues and discussion questions you will cover.
- Pray for the session and for your group members.

Key Scripture
"Let us consider how to provoke one another to love and good deeds, not neglecting to meet together, as is the habit of some, but encouraging one another . . ." —Hebrews 10:24-25

Summary of Main Ideas: Chapter 3
- Intentional Faith Development is purposefully learning in community outside of worship in order to deepen our faith and to grow in grace and in the knowledge and love of God. It is a way of life requiring consistency and commitment. It may involve learning in community through belonging to Bible studies, support groups, prayer teams, service or music ministries, or attending retreats or workshops that focus on the spiritual life.
- We learn faith in community because Jesus and the New Testament have taught us to learn this way, and because spirituality cannot be learned alone.

- Learning in community provides accountability in our walk with Christ.
- When we practice Intentional Faith Development, we . . .
  - are changed from the inside out as we come to know God more intimately and follow Christ more closely;
  - become attentive to the presence and working of the Spirit;
  - connect to other Christians and become part of a supportive community;
  - find strength to change direction and make good decisions;
  - give and receive encouragement;
  - and practice caring for one another.
- People resist Intentional Faith Development for a variety of reasons, including
  - lack of familiarity with Scripture or religious terms;
  - fear of not knowing others in the group and of not being accepted;
  - schedules and obligations;
  - beliefs that may be different from others';
  - and a desire for a "quick fix."
- To practice Intentional Faith Development, people must overcome excuses, make time, find a learning community that fits their schedule, and commit themselves to it.
- People who practice Intentional Faith Development are cultivators of the spiritual life as opposed to consumers of religion. They experiment and explore until they find what works for them, and they continually stretch and challenge themselves to reach new levels of growth.

 ## FOCUS POINTS

1. Intentional Faith Development is purposefully learning in community outside of worship in order to deepen our faith and to grow in grace and in the knowledge and love of God. It requires consistency and commitment.
2. We learn faith in community because Jesus and the New Testament have taught us to learn this way, and because spirituality cannot be learned alone.
3. When we practice Intentional Faith Development, we . . .
   - are changed from the inside out as we come to know God more intimately and follow Christ more closely;

- become attentive to the presence and working of the Spirit;
- become part of a supportive community;
- find strength to change direction and make good decisions;
- give and receive encouragement;
- and practice caring for one another.

2. Getting Started
(5 minutes)

Welcome

Opening Prayer

O God, your plan is for us to continue maturing in faith throughout life, and you invite us to actively cooperate with the Holy Spirit in this process. We acknowledge that one of the primary ways we do this is through belonging to a faith-forming community, which helps us to grow in grace and in the knowledge and love of God so that we may follow Christ more nearly in our daily living. We desire this growth, yet sometimes we allow the busyness and distractions of life to keep us from being intentional about pursuing it. Help us to make room in our lives for learning faith, and give us the commitment and consistency we need to overcome the obstacles. In Jesus' name we pray. Amen.

Scripture / Focus Points

Direct participants' attention to the key Scripture and focus points. You may read them aloud, or have a group member do so, if you choose.

3. Digging In
(25–30 minutes)

Note: More material is provided than you will be able to cover in 25–30 minutes. In advance of the session, select the leader cues and discussion questions you will include and put a checkmark beside them.

FOCUS POINT #1:

Intentional Faith Development is purposefully learning in community outside of worship in order to deepen our faith and to grow in grace and in the knowledge and love of God. It requires consistency and commitment.

Leader Cue

Direct participants to p. 69 in *Five Practices of Fruitful Living*. Read aloud the second full paragraph, which begins, *"Faith development refers to how we purposefully* learn in community *outside of worship. . . ."*

Emphasize the point that faith development is our active cooperation with the Holy Spirit in our own spiritual growth, which takes place as we belong to a faith-forming community.

Group Discussion

- Why do you think spiritual growth requires our active cooperation with the Holy Spirit? Why do you think belonging to a faith-forming community is an important part of this process?
- When have you belonged to a Bible study, class, or other group that helped you to mature in faith and to follow Christ more closely? How would you describe your experience in this faith-forming community?

Leader Cue

Have participants turn to p. 70. (Pause briefly, giving them time to scan the page.) Highlight the importance of being intentional when it comes to faith development. Explain that the word "intentional" derives from Latin words meaning *to stretch out for, to aim at*.

Say: *"Paul describes this yearning for greater fullness in Philippians 3:13-14."* Have someone read the verses aloud.

Note that Intentional Faith Development involves having a plan and being committed and consistent. It requires us to make room in our lives for learning faith—to plan to feed our spirits.

Have participants flip back to p. 69. Ask someone to read aloud "By Prearrangement With Myself."

Group Discussion
- Why do you think it is important to be intentional about faith development?
- How do you make room in your life for faith development? How are you intentional about feeding your spirit?

 FOCUS POINT #2:

We learn faith in community because Jesus and the New Testament have taught us to learn this way, and because spirituality cannot be learned alone.

Leader Cue
Direct participants to p. 71, and have someone read the first two paragraphs aloud.

Group Discussion
- How did Jesus model and teach the practice of learning in community?
- How did the early church continue the practice of learning in community? What were some of the benefits of this practice?

Leader Cue
Emphasize the importance of community to spiritual growth by making the following statements:

> *"The spiritual life is never a solitary affair."* (p. 71)
>
> *"Community provides the catalyst for growth in Christ."* (p. 72)
>
> Then have someone read aloud "Solitary Religion Cannot Subsist at All" (middle of p. 72).

Group Discussion

- Why do you think community is critical to the spiritual life?
- How has community been a catalyst for your own spiritual growth? How have you "discovered Christ" in community?

 FOCUS POINT #3:

When we practice Intentional Faith Development, we . . .
- **are changed from the inside out as we come to know God more intimately and follow Christ more closely;**
- **become attentive to the presence and working of the Spirit;**
- **become part of a supportive community;**
- **find strength to change direction and make good decisions;**
- **give and receive encouragement;**
- **and practice caring for one another.**

Leader Cue

Direct participants to pp. 74–75. Have someone read aloud 2 Timothy 3:16. Then highlight the following points:

- When we read, study, and discuss Scripture together, the Spirit of God works through the conversation, penetrating, enlightening, healing, provoking, correcting, reminding, and reconciling.
- As we consistently meet to study and discuss Scripture in community, we are changed. The transformation may be gradual, but it is significant and life-changing.

- The fruit of Intentional Faith Development is not merely knowing more about God, but knowing God more intimately and following Christ more closely.

Group Discussion

- How has participating in a faith-forming community helped you to know God more intimately and to follow Christ more closely?
- In what ways has this changed you—whether subtly or dramatically?

Leader Cue

Direct participants to the section on "Spiritual Awareness," pp. 75–77. Read aloud the following excerpts:

"When we open Scripture, belong to a community of Christ, and start to explore life with God, we detect God's presence and activity that we never before noticed. A new world opens. . . . We learn to see God."

"Without intentionally cultivating faith, we go through life self-blinded, seeing only a portion of what is before us. We perceive the world through cultural filters that make it nearly impossible to see what is really most important. . . . Learning in community opens our eyes."

Ask someone to read aloud Luke 4:18.

Group Discussion

- How has regular Bible study with others "opened your eyes"?
- What keeps you aware of the spiritual dimension in your daily life? How have you learned to see God in fresh ways?

Leader Cue

Direct participants to p. 77. Note that because many communities and congregations are too large for people to know others well, it is in the intimacy of small groups that we come to feel connected.

Have participants turn to p. 78, and point out that all of us experience challenges and difficulties in life—from common setbacks to more devastating losses. Ask someone to read aloud the second full paragraph, beginning, *"We overestimate our capacity to handle these things all by ourselves, . . ."*

Restate this point for emphasis: *"Belonging to a caring community, we discover a sustenance that does not answer all our questions or end all our challenges, but which keeps us connected, rooted, grounded."*

Summarize with these sentences: *"Community pulls us out of ourselves and carries us toward God"* (p. 79). *"Communion with one another deepens our communion to God"* (p. 77).

Group Discussion
- When was a time when you or a member of your group helped sustain another person during a time of difficulty or grief? What did you learn about yourself through the experience? What did you learn about Christ?
- Why do you think that communion with one another deepens our communion to God?

Leader Cue
Have participants turn to p. 80. Read aloud the first and last sentences of the section "Moral Resolve."

Group Discussion
- How have brothers and sisters in Christ helped to keep you from falling? And when you have fallen, how have they helped to pick you up?

Leader Cue
Direct participants' attention to the section on "Spiritual Encouragement" at the bottom of p. 80. Explain that the word "encouragement" literally means *to put courage into* or *to give heart*. Note that the encouragement of Christian friends helps us to follow Christ more eagerly and boldly.

Group Discussion

- Describe a time when you were encouraged (whether directly or indirectly) by friends in a faith community to follow Christ more closely, eagerly, or boldly.

Leader Cue

Have participants turn to p. 82, and ask someone to read the paragraph beginning, *"God has hard-wired us for belonging; . . ."*

Group Discussion

- Tell of an experience with others that helped to teach you how to give or receive love.
- Respond to this statement: If we want to stay connected to Christ, we must stay connected to one another.
- How has God "fed" your spirit through community?

4. Making Application
(15–20 minutes)

What Does It Look Like?

Direct participants to p. 79. Have someone read aloud the paragraph in the middle of the page, beginning, *"I remember visiting a woman whose husband had died a few months before."*

Briefly discuss:
- How did becoming part of a faith community change this woman?
- What specific actions did she take to become involved?

Have participants flip to the section "The Practice of Intentional Faith Development," beginning on p. 84. Point out that Intentional Faith Development requires commitment and persistence and must be tailored to fit the learning style and temperament of the individual. Then highlight the habits of people who practice Intentional Faith Development.

People who practice Intentional Faith Development . . .
- Experiment and explore until they find what works for them.

- Ask questions such as "What is God teaching me or calling me to change?" in order to connect God to life.
- Move beyond consumer religion to a deeper spiritual life.
- Teach their children about spiritual matters and cultivate a home environment that encourages spiritual development.
- Are free to be themselves, enjoying laughter and love.
- Stretch and challenge themselves to continue learning and growing.
- Develop faith in solitude by reading, reflection, and prayer.
- Love and care for others in community.
- Recommit regularly to new learning opportunities.
- Realize that they will always have more to learn.
- Continually grow in grace and in the knowledge and love of God.

Ask:
- When it comes to Intentional Faith Development, what fits your temperament and learning style? What works for you?
- What are you curious about in the spiritual life at this time? What are you doing to explore faith more deeply?

What Are the Obstacles?

Acknowledge that there are many obstacles or resistances to Intentional Faith Development (see pp. 82–84). Briefly review the following reasons people often resist participating:

- Fear of feeling inadequate or embarrassed by lack of familiarity with Scripture or religious terms
- Awkwardness and intimidation (worrying about not fitting in or being accepted)
- Not knowing anyone in the group
- Time—busy schedules and other obligations
- Beliefs that are different from others' in the group
- Desire for a quick fix

Briefly discuss:
- What has kept you from pursuing or practicing Intentional Faith Development in the past? How did you overcome these obstacles?

What Now?

Instruct participants to reflect silently in response to this question:

- In light of all we have shared today, what do you sense God saying to you?

(Allow 15–20 seconds for reflection.)

End by inviting each participant to share short, "popcorn" answers to these questions:

- In response, what will you do differently this week?
- How will what you learned this week change how you live your life?

As participants prepare to leave, ask them to take time in the coming days to journal or silently meditate on the following questions. You may wish to write these on a board or chart or slips of paper to hand out to each participant. Invite them to share their thoughts or ideas with a prayer partner, family member, friend, or classmate as they are comfortable:

- What would a more dedicated, intentional faith life look like for me?
- Thinking about the next 3–5 years, what patterns do I hope God will use to reshape my life? How will I begin these patterns/practices?

Loving and Serving Others

The Practice of Risk-Taking Mission and Service

1. Getting Ready
(Prior to the Session)

Preparation
- Read Chapter 4 in *Five Practices of Fruitful Living*.
- Write the key Scripture and focus points on a board or chart.
- Review *Digging In* and *Making Application*, and select the leader cues and discussion questions you will cover.
- Pray for the session and for your group members.

Key Scripture
"Then Jesus went to work on his disciples. . . . 'Don't run from suffering; embrace it. Follow me and I'll show you how. Self-help is no help at all. Self-sacrifice is the way, my way, to finding yourself, your true self.' "
—*Matthew 16:24-25*, The Message

Summary of Main Ideas: Chapter 4
- A critical key to a life that is satisfying and rich in purpose involves serving others and making a difference in the world.
- There are various common motivations for serving others:
  1. A sense of duty, obligation, and responsibility
  2. A realization that helping others contributes to the social fabric of human life (I help you; you help me)
  3. A sense of personal satisfaction

  The Holy Spirit purifies all of these motivations when we serve others with the right spirit and focus, respecting others as we serve the purposes of Christ.

- God's call to service/ministry is "the place where your deep gladness and the world's deep hunger meet" (Frederick Buechner, *Wishful Thinking*).[2]
- In Christ, we discover that the truest reality of all is that we are interconnected, that our futures are intertwined, and that we are ultimately one. We belong to one another because we all belong to God.
- We discover ourselves and become the persons God created us to be when we give ourselves to others in Christ-like service.
- We become competent and effective in mission and service through sustained effort—through consistent, repeated, and focused action.
- Risk-Taking Mission and Service changes lives—both of those who offer service and of those who receive it—and transforms the world.
- The practice of Risk-Taking Mission and Service pushes us out of our comfort zone and into places we would never go on our own, which involves learning to overcome fear.
- People who practice Risk-Taking Mission and Service also discern God's call to involve themselves in social change, political activity, and community causes.

 FOCUS POINTS

1. There are various common motivations for serving others, and the Holy Spirit purifies them all when we serve with the right spirit and focus, serving the purposes of Christ.
2. In Christ, we discover that we are all interconnected; we belong to one another because we belong to God.
3. We discover ourselves and become the persons God created us to be when we give ourselves to others in Christ-like service.
4. Risk-Taking Mission and Service changes lives and transforms the world.
5. The practice of Risk-Taking Mission and Service pushes us out of our comfort zone and into places we would never go on our own, which involves learning to overcome fear.

2. Getting Started
(5 minutes)

Welcome

Opening Prayer

Compassionate and loving God, you have designed us in such a way that we discover our true selves when we give ourselves to others. Your own Son, Jesus, modeled this way of living for us. He came to serve, not to be served, and he even gave his life for us. Help us to follow him and devote our lives to serving others with compassion. There is risk and sacrifice involved, which is why we need to be reminded that opening ourselves in this way is not irresponsible but life-giving. Abundant life is found in following you and in giving of ourselves. Help us to match our skills and gifts and interests with specific needs and areas of service, and use us to accomplish your work, transforming lives and the world. Amen.

Scripture / Focus Points

Direct participants' attention to the key Scripture and focus points. You may read them aloud, or have a group member do so, if you choose.

3. Digging In
(25–30 minutes)

Note: More material is provided than you will be able to cover in 25–30 minutes. In advance of the session, select the leader cues and discussion questions you will include and put a checkmark beside them.

 ## FOCUS POINT #1:

There are various common motivations for serving others, and the Holy Spirit purifies them all when we serve with the right spirit and focus, serving the purposes of Christ.

Leader Cue

Begin by pointing out that we tend to live to ourselves. We are focused on our private concerns, personal passions, hobbies, entertainments, family responsibilities, and work obligations. The culture in which we live bombards us with messages such as "Look out for number one," "Love yourself first," and "People are responsible for their own misfortunes."

Direct participants to the bottom of p. 88 in *Five Practices of Fruitful Living* and read the following quotation aloud: *"Most people, given the choice between having a better world, or a better place within the world as it is, would choose the latter."*

Group Discussion

- Given our self-centered tendencies, how do you think anyone learns to serve? How did you learn to serve?
- What's your earliest memory of helping others as an expression of your faith?

Leader Cue

Have participants turn to pp. 89–90. Briefly review the common motivations people can have for serving others. Point out that the Holy Spirit purifies all of these motivations when our genuine desire is to meet the needs of others with respect and humbly serve the purposes of Christ.

Begin reading aloud with the paragraph that begins, *"Need-focused service and passion-driven commitment do not necessarily conflict"* (bottom half of p. 90), and continue to the end of the section (top of p. 91).

Group Discussion

- What motivates you to serve? Do you delight in doing good?
- Where do the world's unmet needs intersect with your own personal passions? What particular gifts, abilities, or

experiences prepare you to make a positive difference—personally, in your community, and in the world?

 ## Focus Point #2:

In Christ, we discover that we are all interconnected; we belong to one another because we belong to God.

Leader Cue

Direct participants to p. 91. Read aloud the first sentence under the heading "Inner Decision": *"Philosophers ponder the question of why a stranger walking by a burning building and hearing the cry of someone inside would put his life at risk to enter the building to try to save a person he does not know."*

Present the idea that we are all interconnected, and that when we come to this realization, we are propelled to the highest and truest of responses. If we allow the person in the burning building to die, something within us dies.

Group Discussion

- Think of a time when you responded to the need of a stranger or someone you did not know well. What prompted you to help? Did you experience a sense of connection with the individual? Describe how you felt during and after the experience.
- What are some small ways you pour out your life to others each day?

 ## Focus Point #3:

We discover ourselves and become the persons God created us to be when we give ourselves to others in Christ-like service.

Leader Cue

Have someone read aloud the following Scriptures: Romans 14:7-8; Matthew 20:27-28; Matthew 25:40; and Mark 8:35.

Then read aloud the following quote from p. 93: *"Serving others does not merely involve helpful activities that make a difference; Christlike service helps us become the persons God created us to be."*

Group Discussion

- How does Christ-like service help us to become the persons God created us to be?
- What experiences of serving have helped you to discover your true self?

Leader Cue

Have participants turn to p. 95 and prepare to read the last paragraph of the section, which precedes the heading "One Person." If space and environment are conducive to the exercise and participants are able and willing, have them lie down on their backs with their arms outstretched as you read the first two sentences of the paragraph. Invite them to do as the woman did, remaining in that position in a mood of exploring prayer as they think about how they feel in that position. After 30–60 seconds of silence, continue reading the remainder of the paragraph. If you choose not to do the exercise, invite participants to close their eyes and imagine they are lying in that position as you read.

Group Discussion

- In what ways have you opened yourself to vulnerability and risk by serving others?
- Do you believe you have discovered greater meaning and abundance as a result of opening yourself to others? Why or why not?

FOCUS POINT #4:

Risk-Taking Mission and Service changes lives and transforms the world.

Leader Cue
Ask participants to turn to pp. 96–97, and briefly review the example of Jennifer to illustrate how one person can make a substantial difference.

Group Discussion
- How does God multiply our efforts, interweaving them with the work of others, to transform the world? Share a way that God has multiplied your efforts to make a difference.
- What does it mean to say that effective service requires practice and persistence?
- How does consistent practice make serving a part of our identity? How has consistent serving helped to shape your identity and direction in life? How has it added to your sense of satisfaction in life?

 # FOCUS POINT #5:

The practice of Risk-Taking Mission and Service pushes us out of our comfort zone and into places we would never go on our own, which involves learning to overcome fear.

Leader Cue
Direct participants to the section "Risk-Taking: Overcoming Fear With Love," which begins on p. 102. Read aloud the following excerpt:

"At the moment we face human suffering, a choice presents itself. If we pay careful attention to our natural tendencies, we discover that we desire to move away. . . . Fear and anxiety move us to secure and predictable territory. [But] if we listen deep within our soul, we discover that

> *something inside us also draws us* toward *the suffering. Every human soul that harbors the tendency to avoid suffering also houses the capacity to respond compassionately."* (p. 104)
>
> Point out that when we choose to respond compassionately, we open ourselves to uncertainty. Practicing Risk-Taking Mission and Service pushes us out of our comfort zone. It requires us to take risks, following where Jesus leads even when it is uncomfortable, awkward, unexpected, and costly.
>
> End with the following statement: *"Training the heart to follow Christ involves learning to overcome fear."* (p. 105)

Group Discussion
- When have you moved out of your "comfort zone" in order to help another person?
- What has been "risk-taking" about your service to Christ?
- What helps you to overcome your fears so that you may follow Christ regardless of the risks or cost?

4. Making Application
(15–20 minutes)

What Does It Look Like?
Have participants turn to the section "Training the Heart," beginning on p. 99. Choose 2-3 of the stories presented in this section and present them briefly (e.g, Ken, Shirley, Ana, Lance, Ruth, Earl, Jan, Sondra).

Briefly discuss:
- How did each of these persons respond to an invitation? What action did they take? How did their actions affect or change others?

Now direct participants to the section "The Practice of Risk-Taking Mission and Service," beginning on p. 109. Highlight the habits or characteristics of people who practice Risk-Taking Mission and Service.

People who practice Risk-Taking Mission and Service . . .
- Go where Jesus goes.
- Are strategic in their service to have a greater impact.
- Focus on the people being served.
- Saturate their work with prayer.
- Practice humility.
- Live out their spiritual convictions.
- Treat others the way they would want to be treated.
- Serve expecting nothing in return, including recognition.
- Practice serving until they feel confident and natural doing it.
- Hold onto hope and never give up.
- Walk gently with those who are vulnerable.
- Collaborate with others to get the job done.
- Immerse themselves in community.
- Take on the hard tasks and find a way.
- Accept the uncertainty of outcomes and take setbacks in stride.
- Teach the next generation how to serve.
- Mobilize others.
- Invite feedback.
- Honor service in many forms—those who are out front and those who work behind the scenes.

Ask:
- Why do you think these habits are critical to effective service?
- Which habits are more challenging for you, and why?

What Are the Obstacles?

Acknowledge that there are many obstacles or resistances to Risk-Taking Mission and Service, including a reluctance or unwillingness to:

- step out and take risks
- make sacrifices

- enter into someone else's pain
- make a significant time investment or ongoing commitment
- open oneself to uncertain or vulnerable circumstances and outcomes

Briefly discuss these obstacles, and invite participants to name any others.

Ask:
- What is the greatest obstacle or challenge to you personally when it comes to Risk-Taking Mission and Service? What would help you to overcome this obstacle?

What Now?

Instruct participants to reflect silently in response to this question:

- In light of all we have shared today, what do you sense God saying to you?

(Allow 15–20 seconds for reflection.)

End by inviting each participant to share short, "popcorn" answers to these questions:

- In response, what will you do differently this week?
- How will what you learned this week change how you live your life?

As participants prepare to leave, ask them to take time in the coming days to journal or silently meditate on the following questions. You may wish to write these on a board or chart or slips of paper to hand out to each participant. Invite them to share their thoughts or ideas with a prayer partner, family member, friend, or classmate as they are comfortable:

- What is "risk-taking" about my service to those in my community, in my world?
- Thinking about the next 3–5 years, what patterns do I hope God will use to reshape my life? How will I begin these patterns/practices?

The Grace of Giving

The Practice of Extravagant Generosity

1. Getting Ready
(Prior to the Session)

Preparation
- Read Chapter 5 in *Five Practices of Fruitful Living*.
- Write the key Scripture and focus points on a board or chart.
- Review *Digging In* and *Making Application*, and select the leader cues and discussion questions you will cover.
- Pray for the session and for your group members.

Key Scripture
"This most generous God who gives seed to the farmer that becomes bread for your meals is more than extravagant with you. He gives you something you can then give away, which grows into full-formed lives, robust in God, wealthy in every way, so that you can be generous in every way."
—*2 Corinthians 9:11*, The Message

Summary of Main Ideas: Chapter 5
- Giving helps us to become what God wants us to be.
- Giving reveals and fosters trust in God.
- The root of generosity is God's love. Knowing God and experiencing God's love lead to generosity.
- Generosity helps us to flourish by
  - aligning us with God's purposes
  - changing us inside
  - mirroring God's nature
  - fostering a healthy relationship to money

 - encouraging intentionality
 - deepening our relationship with God
 - honoring Christ's sacrifice

- The realization that all that we are comes from God and belongs to God leads us to the practice of Extravagant Generosity. This issue of ownership undergirds our theology of giving. We either believe that our material resources belong to God, and we are to manage them for God's purposes, or that they belong to us, and we can do with them as we please. Those who operate from the perspective of a steward find greater happiness.

- Generosity results from a reorientation in our thinking about how we find contentment in life. Contentment is determined by inner spiritual qualities, not by outward circumstances, visible achievements, or material comforts.

- Tithing is a way of putting God first; it is an outward sign of an inner spiritual alignment.

 ## Focus Points

1. The root of generosity is God's love. Knowing God and experiencing God's love lead to generosity.
2. Generosity helps us to flourish by
   - aligning us with God's purposes
   - changing us inside
   - mirroring God's nature
   - fostering a healthy relationship to money
   - encouraging intentionality
   - deepening our relationship with God
   - honoring Christ's sacrifice
3. The realization that all that we are comes from God and belongs to God leads us to the practice of Extravagant Generosity. Those who operate from this perspective—that of a steward—find greater happiness.
4. Generosity results from a reorientation in our thinking about how we find contentment in life. Contentment is determined by inner spiritual qualities, not by outward circumstances, visible achievements, or material comforts.
5. Tithing is a way of putting God first; it is an outward sign of an inner spiritual alignment.

2. Getting Started
(5 minutes)

Welcome

Opening Prayer

Lord, we acknowledge that you are Creator of heaven and earth, and that all things come from you. You have been extravagantly generous with us, giving even your own Son who, though he was rich, became poor so that we might become rich. You are a generous, giving God; it is your very nature. And we acknowledge that because we were made in your image, we, too, have your generous nature imprinted on our souls. You have hard-wired us to be generous, and it is when we live out of this giving nature that we find contentment and freedom. Help us listen to the promptings of your Spirit rather than the pressures of our culture so that, in the words of John Wesley, we may "do all the good [we] can, by all the means [we] can, in all the ways [we] can, in all the places [we] can, to all the people [we] can, as long as ever [we] can." Amen.

Scripture / Focus Points

Direct participants' attention to the key Scripture and focus points. You may read them aloud, or have a group member do so, if you choose.

3. Digging In
(25–30 minutes)

Note: More material is provided than you will be able to cover in 25–30 minutes. In advance of the session, select the leader cues and discussion questions you will include and put a checkmark beside them.

 FOCUS POINT #1:

The root of generosity is God's love. Knowing God and experiencing God's love lead to generosity.

Leader Cue

Direct participants to pp. 117–118 in *Five Practices of Fruitful Living*. Note that the root of generosity is God's love, and that because of God's great love for us, God has been extravagantly generous on our behalf. Have several participants read aloud the following Scriptures: John 3:16; Romans 11:33-36; and 2 Corinthians 8:9.

Group Discussion

- How has God been generous on our behalf?
- How has God been generous to you personally?

Leader Cue

Read aloud the following excerpt from p. 119: *"No stories from Scripture tell of people living the God-related spiritual life while fostering a greedy, self-centered, self-serving attitude. Knowing God leads to generosity."*

Group Discussion

- Does knowing God and experiencing God's love and generosity motivate you to give? Explain your response.
- How does giving shape your relationship to God?

 FOCUS POINT #2:

Generosity helps us to flourish by
- **aligning us with God's purposes**
- **changing us inside**
- **mirroring God's nature**
- **fostering a healthy relationship to money**
- **encouraging intentionality**
- **deepening our relationship with God**
- **honoring Christ's sacrifice**

Leader Cue

Direct participants' attention to pp. 119–125. Briefly review the ways that generosity helps us to flourish. Touch on the following highlights:

- Our giving makes God's work in the world possible. When we give, we align ourselves with God's purposes.
- When we give, our motivations change and we are drawn closer to God.
- Because God is generous and we are made in the image of God, generosity is part of our essential nature.
- Being intentional about giving helps us to keep our priorities straight. When we put God first rather than succumb to the influences of culture, which only make us discontent, money becomes a servant rather than our master.
- Giving helps us to become more intentional about how we manage and spend our money, causing us to reflect more deeply on questions related to purpose and happiness.
- Giving intensifies our love for the things God loves, feeding our love for God and deepening our relationship with God.
- Giving honors Christ by allowing us to participate in the ultimate self-giving nature we perceive in the life, death, and resurrection of Christ.

Group Discussion

- What difference has the practice of giving made in your life? How has it helped you to flourish?

 FOCUS POINT #3:

The realization that all that we are comes from God and belongs to God leads us to the practice of Extravagant Generosity. Those who operate from this perspective—that of a steward—find greater happiness.

Leader Cue

Have someone read aloud Romans 11:33-36 a second time. Then ask participants to turn to p. 125, and have someone read aloud the second and third paragraphs under the heading "Ownership."

Group Discussion

- Which of these two views is truest? How close are you to living out the first view?

Leader Cue

Share the example of the possession of land found on p. 126.

Group Discussion

- Does the idea that you are a temporary beneficiary motivate you to use what God has entrusted to you to the highest purposes? Why or why not?
- How can this perspective help us to make better decisions and deepen our spiritual sense of community and responsibility?
- Tell about a time when operating from the perspective of a "steward" (as opposed to an "owner") gave you a sense of satisfaction, fulfillment, or happiness.

 FOCUS POINT #4:

Generosity results from a reorientation in our thinking about how we find contentment in life. Contentment is determined by inner spiritual qualities, not by outward circumstances, visible achievements, or material comforts.

Leader Cue

Have someone read aloud Philippians 4:11. Then share the following excerpts:

"Despite the fact that we live in better houses, earn more money, drive nicer cars, spend more on entertainment, and enjoy greater conveniences than ninety percent of the world's population, or than we ourselves enjoyed thirty years ago, we never have enough." (p. 122)

"Even possessing greater wealth and finer houses than most of the world does not mean that we experience contentedness. We can still feel panic, emptiness, striving, and isolation. When we base our self-worth on our salary, or on which neighborhood we live in, or what type of car we drive, then we race for more 'meaning' by having more possessions. We feel needy, and our appetites become insatiable. . . . Breaking the cycle of conditioned discontent requires courageous soul work. It takes knowledge, insight, and the support of others to handle this from deep inside. The inner life shapes how we feel, what we value, and our attitude toward possessions. Contentment arises from seeking that which satisfies." (p. 127)

Group Discussion

- How have you been conditioned by cultural influences to be discontent?
- What causes you to feel content? What truly satisfies your deepest longings for acceptance, approval, and happiness?

Leader Cue

Have participants turn to p. 128 and review the four ways that contentedness is formed in us:

- The practice of generosity
- A deep, cultivated sense of gratitude
- The spiritual awareness that God has provided all we need
- Persistent interior work and cooperation with the Holy Spirit

---

Group Discussion

- How difficult is it for you to choose to give rather than merely acquire? How is giving a part of your life?

- Do you tend to have an attitude of gratitude? What can help us to "give thanks in all things" as the Apostle Paul instructs in 1 Thessalonians 5:18?
- How successful are you in living within your means? What might you do to live below your means? How might you live more simply?
- What personal habits tend to cause you to give in to the pressure of materialism? What habits help to keep you grounded and to sustain a sense of contentedness?

 ## FOCUS POINT #5:

Tithing is a way of putting God first; it is an outward sign of an inner spiritual alignment.

Leader Cue

Direct participants to p. 129 and review the concept of tithing. Point out that Jesus commended the practice, and that the early church practiced the tithe—as have Christians in every generation since. Then read aloud the following excerpts:

"Tithing provides a concrete way for us to take the words we speak, 'God is Lord of my life,' and put them into practice. Our commitment becomes tangible; our giving becomes a way of putting God first, an outward sign of an inner spiritual alignment." (p. 130)

"Tithing is not merely a financial decision; it is a life choice that rearranges all the furniture of our interior lives." (p. 131)

"We have trouble tithing today because we live in more affluent times, and we have allowed our affluence to shape us more than our faith." (p. 131)

Group Discussion

- How do you feel about tithing? Do you practice proportional giving or tithing? If so, why? If not, why not?

- When was a time you felt God's Spirit move you to give your resources beyond what you had previously practiced?

4. Making Application
(15–20 minutes)

What Does It Look Like?
Have participants turn to pp. 115–116. Briefly retell the story of Terri and Charles, summarizing the highlights.

Discuss:
- How would you describe Terri and Charles' life before they began the journey to change their lifestyle so that they could pay off debt, save, and give more? How would you describe their life after?
- What were some of the specific decisions and changes they made along the way?

Direct participants to the section "The Practice of Extravagant Generosity," beginning on p. 133. Highlight the habits or characteristics of people who practice Extravagant Generosity.

People who practice Extravagant Generosity . . .
- Make giving a priority.
- Give generously and enthusiastically.
- Change their lives in order to become more generous.
- Are intentional in their giving, supporting ministries marked by fruitfulness and excellence and expecting accountability and transparency.
- Grow in the grace of giving, continuing to give more and more.
- Push their congregations to become more generous.
- See needs and step forward to meet them without being asked.
- Give with conviction and humility.
- Motivate and teach others to give, including their children and grandchildren.
- Give out of present income and occasionally from investments for major projects.

- Look at difficult financial times through the eyes of faith rather than fear, giving in all seasons.
- View personal success as a reason to share.
- Give expecting nothing in return, including recognition.
- Are content with what they have and find satisfaction in simpler things, avoiding debt and waste.
- Live with a sense of gratitude.
- Give generously beyond their church.
- Enjoy giving.

Ask:

- Why do you think these habits are critical to Extravagant Generosity?
- Which habits are more challenging for you, and why?

What Are the Obstacles?

Acknowledge that there are many obstacles or resistances to Extravagant Generosity, including

- the fear of giving up things that give us pleasure
- the spiritual work, practical planning, and intentionality required
- the idea that we will give when a financial break frees us to be generous
- a lack of support from family members
- the mindset that our spiritual lives are separate from what we do with our finances

Briefly discuss these obstacles, and invite participants to name any others.

Ask:

- What obstacles prevent you from giving extravagantly?
- What is the greatest obstacle or challenge, and what would help you to overcome it?

What Now?

Instruct participants to reflect silently in response to this question:

- In light of all we have shared today, what do you sense God saying to you?

(Allow 15–20 seconds for reflection.)

End by inviting each participant to share short, "popcorn" answers to these questions:

- In response, what will you do differently this week?
- How will what you learned this week change how you live your life?

As participants prepare to leave, ask them to take time in the coming days to journal or silently meditate on the following questions. You may wish to write these on a board or chart or slips of paper to hand out to each participant. Invite them to share their thoughts or ideas with a prayer partner, family member, friend, or classmate as they are comfortable:

- How does giving shape my relationship to God? How can my giving become more extravagant?
- Thinking about the next 3–5 years, what patterns do I hope God will use to reshape my life? How will I begin these patterns/practices?

Fruitful Living and Offering God's Love

1. Getting Ready
(Prior to the Session)

Preparation
- Read Chapter 6 in *Five Practices of Fruitful Living*.
- Write the key Scripture and focus points on a board or chart.
- Review *Digging In* and *Making Application*, and select the leader cues and discussion questions you will cover.
- Pray for the session and for your group members.

Key Scripture
"Be ready to speak up and tell anyone who asks why you're living the way you are, and always with the utmost courtesy." —1 Peter 3:15, The Message

Summary of Main Ideas: Chapter 6
- Disciples of Jesus Christ bear fruit—both in their interior lives and in outward attitudes and behaviors.
- Radical Hospitality, Passionate Worship, Intentional Faith Development, Risk-Taking Mission and Service, and Extravagant Generosity are the practices of fruitful living. Fruitful living changes us inside and, through us, transforms the world for God's purposes.
- Living fruitfully involves inviting others to Christ (communicating the love of God and offering God's grace). As disciples, this is our mission, and this mission completes us.

- The church fulfills its mission at the margins of the congregation, where those who actively follow Christ encounter those who are not a part of the community of faith.
- The purpose of inviting others to follow Jesus is to help them rediscover God's love and to provide a community that gives sustained focus, energy, and resources to developing the spiritual life.
- To bear witness to Christ involves more than inviting people with words; it means living with such grace and integrity that our lives themselves become appealing to others. Witness is a way of life that invites God to work through us.

 ## FOCUS POINTS

1. Disciples of Jesus Christ bear fruit. Fruitful living changes us inside and, through us, transforms the world for God's purposes.
2. Living fruitfully involves inviting others to Christ (communicating the love of God and offering God's grace). As disciples, this is our mission, and this mission completes us.
3. The church fulfills its mission at the margins of the congregation where those who actively follow Christ encounter those who are not part of the community of faith.
4. To bear witness to Christ involves more than inviting people with words; it is a way of life that invites God to work through us. Radical Hospitality toward God becomes Radical Hospitality toward others.

2. Getting Started
(5 minutes)

Welcome

Opening Prayer

Jesus, you have called us, your disciples, to bear much fruit. We do this by cultivating the fruit of the Spirit—love, joy, peace, patience, kindness, generosity, faithfulness, gentleness, and self-control—and by practicing the habits that lead to fruitful living. We have been studying these habits for the past several weeks—Radical Hospitality, Passionate Worship, Intentional Faith Development, Risk-Taking Mission and Service, and Extravagant Generosity. There is one thing that multiplies these habits more than anything else, and it is offering your love to others and inviting them to the spiritual life. In fact, this is our mission as your disciples. We are your ambassadors. Help us to overcome our discomfort, objections, and fears that keep us from inviting others to experience your love. May we invite others not only with our words, but also with our very lives, making others want to live like us. Amen.

Scripture / Focus Points

Direct participants' attention to the key Scripture and focus points. You may read them aloud, or have a group member do so, if you choose.

3. Digging In
(25–30 minutes)

Note: More material is provided than you will be able to cover in 25–30 minutes. In advance of the session, select the leader cues and discussion questions you will include and put a checkmark beside them.

 FOCUS POINT #1:

Disciples of Jesus Christ bear fruit. Fruitful living changes us inside and, through us, transforms the world for God's purposes.

Leader Cue

Have someone read aloud John 15:8; Luke 10:1-2; Matthew 13:31; and Galatians 5:22-23.

Group Discussion

- In light of these verses, how would you describe or explain spiritual fruitfulness? What does it mean to live fruitfully?

Leader Cue

Direct participants to p. 140 in *Five Practices of Fruitful Living*. Briefly review the practices of fruitful living: Radical Hospitality, Passionate Worship, Intentional Faith Development, Risk-Taking Mission and Service, and Extravagant Generosity. Talk about how these practices foster inner growth and manifest outward consequence. Note that the first three practices especially feed inner fruitfulness while the others particularly bear fruit in the world around us.

Group Discussion

- What practices of fruitful living are a regular part of your life?
- How have these practices changed you? How have they brought change or transformation through you into the lives of others?

 FOCUS POINT #2:

Living fruitfully involves inviting others to Christ (communicating the love of God and offering God's grace). As disciples, this is our mission, and this mission completes us.

Leader Cue

Read aloud the following four excerpts, calling out the page references in advance so that participants may follow along if they like.

> *"Living fruitfully includes passing along the faith and creating spiritual life in others. . . . Offering God's love so that others may accept God's grace bears fruit beyond what we can fathom. . . . Seeds are scattered, some take root and bear fruit in ways beyond what we can comprehend."* (p. 141)
>
> *"An essential element of our life with Christ involves our finding the courage and the voice to invite others to Christ."* (p. 146)
>
> *"Our* mission *is to communicate the love of God, to offer God's grace. Every follower of Christ becomes part of the mission and is sent out as 'ambassadors of Christ.' "* (p. 147)
>
> *"The initiating and invitational posture is essential to discipleship. Invitation completes us—there are depths of the inner life that remain beyond our experience without offering Christ."* (p. 148)
>
> Ask participants to turn to p. 145 and have someone read aloud "The Most Likely Pathway."

Group Discussion

- Who first offered God's love to you? Who invited you into the community of faith and made you feel welcome? What did they do to create a sense of belonging for you?
- When was a time you felt God moving you toward another person in some spiritual way?
- How have you invited someone to participate in a service or ministry of the church? What made the time ripe for the invitation?

 FOCUS POINT #3:

The church fulfills its mission at the margins of the congregation where those who actively follow Christ encounter those who are not part of the community of faith.

Leader Cue

Direct participants to p. 152. Present the visual concept of a congregation as concentric circles of relationship, with those who know each other well and offer leadership in the middle, those who faithfully volunteer a little farther out, and those who are newer or less active a little farther still. On the other side of the edge of the farthest circle are the people who are not part of the community of faith. (If possible, draw this on a board or chart.)

Then have participants turn to p. 154 and have someone read aloud the two paragraphs, beginning with, *"How do we find our voice, our manner, our way to reach out to others?"* (middle of page), and ending with *"It would change you."*

Conclude with the following statements from p. 156:

"A significant element of [the church's] decline is the personal unwillingness of individual disciples to comfortably and consistently invite others into the community of faith and into the life of Christ. When we pray for renewal for our congregations, we can't ask God to do for us what God created us to do for God."

Group Discussion

- When was a time you had a conversation about the spiritual life with someone who has no church home? How did that feel?
- How did the experience affect them? How did it affect you?

 FOCUS POINT #4:

To bear witness to Christ involves more than inviting people with words; it is a way of life that invites God to work through us. Radical Hospitality toward God becomes Radical Hospitality toward others.

Leader Cue

Direct participants to p. 157. Talk about how love is the key to being a compelling witness for Jesus Christ. Point out that we are to love because God first loved us, and that people are drawn to Christ when we share this love with others. Note that the second chapter of Acts reports that people found the way of life of the followers of Christ to be utterly compelling and irresistibly appealing.

Group Discussion

- What is it about your life that would make someone else want to be a follower of Jesus Christ and be involved in a faith community? Are you living the kind of life that would make others want to live like you?

4. Making Application
(15–20 minutes)

What Does It Look Like?

Direct participants to the story of Mark and Diana on pp. 142–146. Be prepared to summarize the story, noting the highlights.

Briefly discuss:

- How did Tom share God's love with Mark and Diana? What happened as a result of Tom's initial invitation? How did others continue to demonstrate and share the love of God with Mark and Diana? How were they changed as a result?

Have participants flip to the section "Offering God's Love," beginning on p. 159. Highlight the habits or characteristics of people who offer God's love through example and invitation.

People who offer God's love . . .
- Trust God's time, realizing that the journey is a process that begins with personal relationship and giving people space.

- Train themselves to feel comfortable talking about spirituality and the interior life with outsiders.
- Speak with humility, sharing their faith struggles as well as their trust in matters of spirit.
- Pray about particular people who have no faith community, asking God's guidance to notice when the way opens.
- View people through God's eyes, ruling no one out.
- Attend to small actions.
- Believe that the church is the body of Christ and a principal means of grace.
- Sometimes train to offer God's love in unusually hard circumstances.
- Are more concerned about connecting people to Christ than increasing membership numbers.
- Realize that faith is a journey of a thousand incremental steps, and that everyone moves at different paces.
- Allow Christ's invitational nature to pervade all their work
- have an others-centered approach.
- Do not procrastinate, postpone, avoid, resist, or deny the importance of offering God's love.

Ask:
- Why do you think these habits are critical to offering God's love to others?
- Which habits are more challenging for you, and why?

What Are the Obstacles?

Acknowledge that there are many obstacles or resistances to offering God's love, including

- the fear of offending people
- the feeling that we may be imposing our values on others
- the idea that inviting another person into the faith community feels manipulative, artificial, contrived, and utilitarian
- negative stereotypes of evangelism done rudely
- difficulty offering the invitation in a healthy manner that fits our theology and temperament due to a lack of good examples

Briefly discuss these obstacles, and invite participants to name any others.

Ask:
- What obstacles prevent you from offering God's love and inviting others into the faith community?
- What is the greatest obstacle or challenge, and what would help you to overcome it?

What Now?

Instruct participants to reflect silently in response to this question:

- In light of all we have shared today, what do you sense God saying to you?

(Allow 15–20 seconds for reflection.)

End by inviting each participant to share short, "popcorn" answers to these questions:

- In response, what will you do differently this week?
- How will what you learned this week change how you live your life?

As participants prepare to leave, ask them to take time in the coming days to journal or silently meditate on the following questions. You may wish to write these on a board or chart or slips of paper to hand out to each participant. Invite them to share their thoughts or ideas with a prayer partner, family member, friend, or classmate as they are comfortable:

- Do I live a life that would make someone want to follow Christ and be involved in a faith community?
- Thinking about the next 3–5 years, what patterns do I hope God will use to reshape my life? How will I begin these patterns/practices?

90-Minute Group
Session Model

To extend a 60-minute group session to 90 minutes, simply increase the time allowed for *Digging In* by 15 minutes and the time allowed for *Making Application* by 20 minutes. This will allow participants to engage in more in-depth discussion and to give more concerted attention to personal application. The revised model looks like this:

1. Getting Ready
(Prior to the Session)

2. Getting Started
(5 minutes)

3. Digging In
(45 minutes)

Adding 15 minutes of discussion time, extending this segment to a total of 45 minutes, should give you enough time to cover most, if not all, of the leader cues and discussion questions. Keep a watch on the time and be prepared to move ahead more quickly or eliminate a question or two if necessary.

4. Making Application
(40 minutes)

What Does It Look Like? (20 minutes)

Allow 10 minutes for presenting and discussing the real-life example(s), and 10 minutes for reviewing and discussing the common habits or characteristics of people who live out the given practice.

What Are the Obstacles? (15 minutes)

Allow 15 minutes for discussing the obstacles that hinder the implementation of the practice.

What Now? (5 minutes)

Allow a total of 5 minutes for participants to reflect silently on what God has said to them during the session and then to share their "popcorn" responses, indicating what they will do differently in the coming week and in their life overall.

12-Week Model

Groups that have only one hour for the group session (e.g., Sunday school classes) but that would like to have a more in-depth study may opt to extend the study to 12 weeks. To do this, simply divide each session outline into two separate sessions as illustrated by the following example. (This example is a modification of Session 1 found on pp. 19–28.)

Session 1: Receiving God's Love
The Practice of Radical Hospitality

1. Getting Ready
(Prior to the Session)

Preparation
- Read Chapter 1 in *Five Practices of Fruitful Living*.
- Write the key Scripture and focus points on a board or chart.
- Review *Digging In* and *Making Application*, and select the leader cues and discussion questions you will cover.
- Pray for the session and for your group members.

Key Scripture
"We love because he first loved us." —1 John 4:19

Summary of Main Ideas: Chapter 1

- The first step in our walk of faith is saying *Yes* to God's unconditional love for us. In the words of Paul Tillich, we accept that we are accepted, and in that moment we are "struck by grace"[1]—we receive the love and forgiveness of God, begin to comprehend its meaning, and open ourselves to the new life it brings.
- Radical Hospitality involves being receptive to God's love and intentionally making room for God in our lives. It is the key to all the practices that lead to fruitful living.
- Grace is the active, reaching, gift-like quality of God's love. God's grace seeks us and unexpectedly breaks open our hearts, changing us and working its way through us to others.
- Jesus is the ultimate expression of God's grace.
- Faith is our acceptance of God's gift of grace. We receive God's grace, love, and pardon, and allow these gifts to shape us and make us anew.
- There are many obstacles that prevent us from receiving God's love and make us inhospitable to God's initiative; including cultural voices; fast-forward living; negative internal messages; and our own attitudes, choices, and behaviors.
- The good life comes from opening ourselves to God's grace, and often we come to a place of receptivity through unexpected moments or events.

 Focus Points

1. Radical Hospitality involves being receptive to God's love and intentionally making room for God in our lives.
2. Grace is the initiating, gift-like quality of God's love that seeks us and changes us. Jesus is the ultimate expression of God's grace.
3. Faith is our acceptance of God's gift of grace.
4. The good life comes from patterns of opening ourselves to God's grace rather than closing ourselves off from God— from saying *Yes* to the spiritual life rather than *No*—and

often we come to a place of receptivity through unexpected moments or events.

2. Getting Started
(5 minutes)

Welcome

Opening Prayer

Gracious God, you love us unconditionally and accept us unreservedly. Because of your great love for us, you pursue us and break into our lives with the gift of your amazing grace, offering us forgiveness, restoration, wholeness, and abundant life through your Son, Jesus—the ultimate expression of your grace. All we have to do is open ourselves to your love and accept your gift. It is so simple, and yet there are so many voices and distractions that threaten to keep us from being receptive to your love. Help us to overcome these obstacles and to become more receptive to you. Teach us to cultivate the practice of Radical Hospitality in our lives, of opening ourselves again and again to you and making a place in our hearts for your love. In Jesus' name we pray. Amen.

Scripture / Focus Points

Direct participants' attention to the key Scripture and focus points. You may read them aloud, or have a group member do so, if you choose.

3. Digging In
(45 minutes)

This modification of the original session outline adds 15 minutes of discussion time here, extending this segment to a total of 45 minutes. This should give you enough time to cover most, if not all, of the leader cues and discussion questions. Keep a watch on the time and be prepared to move ahead more quickly or eliminate a question or two if necessary.

Focus Point #1:

Radical Hospitality involves being receptive to God's love and intentionally making room for God in our lives.

Leader Cue

Direct participants to p. 17 in *Five Practices of Fruitful Living*. Have someone read the first paragraph aloud.

Now have participants turn to p. 18. Read aloud the following passage (middle of the page), emphasizing the underlined words and pausing as indicated:

"You are <u>loved</u>. [pause] You <u>are</u> loved. [pause] <u>You</u> are loved. [pause]
"Can you accept that?
"God's love for us is not something we have to strive for, earn, work on, or fear. It is freely given. That is key: that we are loved, first, finally, and forever by God, a love so deep and profound and significant that God offers his Son to signify and solidify this love forever so that we get it."

Group Discussion
- How have you felt/experienced God's unconditional love?
- Have you truly accepted that you are loved and accepted by God? If not, what is keeping you from accepting this reality?
- Have you ever felt that you must strive for, earn, or fear God's love? Why?

Leader Cue

Direct participants back to p. 17. Briefly present Tillich's concept of being "struck by grace." Emphasize the following points:

- When God's grace strikes us, we are faced with the startling reality of God's unconditional love for us.
- This realization jars us into a new way of thinking.
- Receiving and understanding the love and forgiveness of God opens us to new life, and this can be as abrupt as lightening and as disruptive as an earthquake.

Group Discussion

- What do you understand the phrase "struck by grace" to mean?
- How have you been struck by God's grace?

Leader Cue

Have participants turn to p. 19. Ask someone to read aloud "Just Say Yes!" found at the bottom of the page.

Group Discussion

- When have you said *Yes* to God when you could have said *No*, and what difference has this made for you?

 ## FOCUS POINT #2:

Grace is the initiating, gift-like quality of God's love that seeks us and changes us. Jesus is the ultimate expression of God's grace.

Leader Cue

Have someone read aloud the key Scripture: 1 John 4:19 (perhaps from a different translation this time), followed by Ephesians 2:8.

Next, read aloud the following excerpt from the bottom of p. 21: *"It's not that we love first, but that we are first loved. This active, reaching quality of God's love is what grace refers to, a gift-like initiative on God's part toward us."*

Group Discussion

- Through what persons, experiences, or events have you encountered the initiating, gift-like quality of God's grace?
- How have you been changed by God's grace?

Leader Cue
Direct participants to p. 23. Read aloud the following excerpts:

"Jesus is the ultimate expression of God's grace, God becoming human in order to reach us and to make possible living abundantly, meaningfully, lovingly, and gracefully."

"The God we see revealed in Jesus is the God of grace, an active, searching, embracing, assertive love."

Highlight some of the descriptions of God's grace as demonstrated through Jesus:
- *strong, persevering, gritty grace*—that embraced untouchables and outcasts
- *courageous grace*—that interceded against violence and injustice on behalf of a woman accused of adultery
- *earthy, practical grace*—that modeled servanthood by washing the disciples' feet
- *unrelenting, irresistible grace*—that never gave up on the hopeless or the powerful
- *disturbing, interruptive grace*—that overturned the tables of the money changers in the Temple
- *perceptive, affirming grace*—that noticed a widow with her two coins and a mourning father
- *compassionate grace*—that embraced victims of violence
- *persistent grace*—that stepped into cell blocks with prisoners
- *challenging, correcting, indicting grace*—that confronted unsympathetic rich people and haughty religious leaders
- *costly, sacrificial grace*—that absorbed the violence of humiliation, unjust persecution, and torturous death to reveal the depth of God's love for humanity

Group Discussion

- How have you seen the active, searching, unrelenting grace of God at work to reach someone with God's love?
- How have you experienced the grace of God through Jesus? How would you describe this grace?

 FOCUS POINT #3:

Faith is our acceptance of God's gift of grace.

Leader Cue

Have someone reread Ephesians 2:8 aloud for the group.

Point out that the apostle Paul said there are two essential and operative elements to a whole and right relationship with God: *grace* and *faith*. Remind participants of the gift analogy found at the bottom of p. 22. Grace is God's gift to us. Faith is our acceptance of God's gift.

Read aloud the following excerpt from the bottom of p. 22: "Faith *is our acceptance of the gift, the opening of our hearts to invite God's love into our lives.* Faith *is our receiving God's grace, love, and pardon, and allowing these gifts to shape us and make us anew.* Faith *is the commitment again and again to live by grace, to honor the gift, and use it, and pass it along."*

Group Discussion

- Why are both grace and faith necessary for a right, whole relationship with God?
- What part has faith played in your practice of Radical Hospitality—your ability to say *Yes* to God and make room for God in your life?

 ## FOCUS POINT #4:

The good life comes from patterns of opening ourselves to God's grace rather than closing ourselves off from God—from saying *Yes* to the spiritual life rather than *No*—and often we come to a place of receptivity through unexpected moments or events.

Leader Cue

Direct participants to p. 33. Read aloud the following excerpt:

"We never earn enough, do enough, or achieve enough to guarantee happiness. We do not become what God created us to be simply by more activity, faster motion, working harder, or having more stuff. . . . And

contrary to self-help books, the good life cannot come from inside us or by our own efforts either. We do not achieve it by trying harder, pushing further, pulling ourselves up by our own bootstraps. . . . The good life comes from the practice of hospitality toward God, opening ourselves to God, and making room in our hearts for the gift-like transformation God's love makes possible."

Briefly review the things mentioned at the bottom of the page that result in the happiness found in "the good life":
- patterns of living that draw us closer to God
- practices that open and reopen the connections that bind us to God and the community
- learning to love and be loved
- serving and being served
- focusing outward, offering ourselves to make a difference

Group Discussion
- Compare the inner happiness that comes from God's Spirit with the happiness defined by culture.
- What personal patterns and practices help you to cultivate the good life?

Leader Cue
Point out that sometimes we are not receptive to God's grace until unexpected situations or experiences break into our interior lives, causing us to ask questions and making us aware of our yearning.

Group Discussion
- What unexpected moments or situations have brought you to a new or deeper receptivity to God and God's grace?

4. Closing
(3–5 minutes)

Tell participants that you will devote the next session to personal application of the practice of Radical Hospitality. In addition to discussing how to implement the practice in everyday life, you will consider some of the common obstacles or resistances to the practice and discuss ways to overcome them.

Close with a time of prayer. You may pray for the group yourself, invite someone else to pray, or allow group members to take turns praying spontaneously as the Spirit leads.

12-Week Model *continued*

Session 2: Receiving God's Love
The Practice of Radical Hospitality

1. Getting Started
(5 minutes)

Welcome

Opening Prayer
Offer an opening prayer.

Scripture / Focus Points
Briefly remind participants of the main topics of discussion from last week's session. One way to do this is to review the key Scripture and focus points once again, reading them aloud and briefly noting any significant comments, insights, or stories shared in the last session.

2. Making Application
(45 minutes)

This modification of the original session outline adds 15 minutes here, extending the time for application to 45 minutes. The group will address three major questions: 1) What does it look like? 2) What are the obstacles? and 3) What now?

You have a total of 40 minutes for addressing the first two questions, and you may divide this time between the two questions as you choose. For example, you might spend 20 minutes discussing each of the first two questions, or you might choose to devote more time to one of the questions and less time to the other. This leaves you with 5 minutes for the final question: What now?

What Does It Look Like? (+/- 20 minutes)

Have participants turn to Mitch's story, beginning on p. 34. Be prepared to summarize the story, noting the highlights.

Discuss:
- What signs of receptivity can you identify in Mitch's story—moments when he could have said *No* but instead said *Yes* to God?

Direct participants to the section "Practicing Radical Hospitality Toward God," beginning on p. 36. Point out that Radical Hospitality involves receptivity and intentional practice. Then highlight the habits of people who practice Radical Hospitality.

People who practice Radical Hospitality . . .
- Look for ways to invite God in.
- Deliberately say *Yes* to promptings of the Spirit.
- Regularly ask for God's help.
- Desire God's presence.
- Make space in their lives and hearts for "soul work."
- Welcome interruptions by God into their lives and see them as opportunities.
- Look for evidence of God's presence and work.
- Seek to know God more and learn new things.
- Allow God to become the fundamental and defining part of their life.

- Practice, repeat, and deepen the core essentials that open themselves to God.
- Say *No* to other things so that they may say *Yes* to God.
- Open themselves to the community of faith.
- Are willing to wrestle with God.
- Are validated by God's love and acceptance.
- Seek first God's kingdom.

Ask:
- How do your present patterns of living invite God in or cause you to avoid the spiritual life?

What Are the Obstacles? (+/- 20 minutes)

Acknowledge that there are many obstacles that prevent us from receiving God's love and make us inhospitable to God's initiative (see pp. 25–32). Highlight the four categories outlined in the book:

- Cultural voices (television, radio, magazines, billboards, the Internet, iPods, cell phones, etc.)
- Fast-forward living (high-tech and highly mobile lifestyles)
- Negative internal messages (negative voices of family members or other influential persons in our lives)
- Our own attitudes, choices, and behaviors (selfishness, self-preoccupation, self-absorption, destructive decisions and habits)

Briefly discuss:
- Which obstacles or distractions keep you from fully receiving God's love?

What Now? (5 minutes)

Instruct participants to reflect silently in response to this question:

- In light of all we have shared today, what do you sense God saying to you?

(Allow 15–20 seconds for reflection.)

End by inviting each participant to share short, "popcorn" answers to these questions:

- In response, what will you do differently this week?
- How will what you learned this week change how you live your life?

As participants prepare to leave, ask them to take time in the coming days to journal or silently meditate on the following questions. You may wish to write these on a board or chart or slips of paper to hand out to each participant. Invite them to share their thoughts or ideas with a prayer partner, family member, friend, or classmate as they are comfortable:

- What would greater receptivity or openness to God look like for my life?
- Thinking about the next 3–5 years, what patterns do I hope God will use to reshape my life? How will I begin these patterns/practices?

3. Closing
(3–5 minutes)

Tell participants that in your next session you will move on to the second of the Five Practices: Passionate Worship.

Close with a time of prayer. You may pray for the group, invite someone else to pray, or allow members to take turns praying spontaneously as the Spirit leads.

APPENDIX C

Weekend Retreat

This weekend retreat model is designed for a Friday evening through Saturday afternoon retreat. Some groups may choose to add additional time either before or after the retreat for leisure/relaxation, fellowship, or other planned activities. Feel free to modify the model for a Saturday-Sunday retreat, beginning with either lunch or dinner on Saturday and concluding at noon or later on Sunday afternoon. You also may use this model on other days of the week with staff or other leadership who are able to get away at that time.

To enhance the experience of learning and community, distribute copies of the book *Five Practices of Fruitful Living* to participants at least two weeks in advance and encourage people to read the book in preparation. To prepare the content of the teaching/learning sessions for each of the practices, refer to the chapter outlines and focus questions in this Leader Guide. Encourage discussion in small groups. If the schedule and setting allow, give time for personal journaling or quiet times of reflection, walking, or leisure between sessions so that participants can absorb the material more personally. Closing worship may include times of sharing about insights people have discovered through the retreat experience, and may include a time of commitment or recommitment to deepening the spiritual life through practice.

Friday Evening

6:00–6:45	Dinner
6:45–7:00	Break

7:00–7:30   Opening Worship

7:30–8:00   Orientation Session (Pull from the orientation session in this Leader Guide, pp. 11–18, and the introduction to *Five Practices of Fruitful Living*)

8:00–8:15   Break

8:15–9:15   Session 1: Radical Hospitality

9:15–9:30   Closing Worship / Prayer

9:30   Free Time

Saturday Morning

7:30–8:30   Breakfast

8:30–9:00   Morning Worship

9:00–10:00   Session 2: Passionate Worship

10:00–10:15 Break

10:15–11:15 Session 3: Intentional Faith Development

11:15–12:30 Lunch / Free Time

Saturday Afternoon

12:30–12:45 Praise and Worship

12:45–1:45   Session 4: Risk-Taking Mission and Service

1:45–2:00   Break

2:00–3:00	Session 5: Extravagant Generosity
3:00–3:30	Free Time or Planned Activity
3:30–4:00	Session 6: Fruitful Living and Offering God's Love
4:00–4:30	Closing Worship / Holy Communion
4:30	Leave for Home

Other Uses

The material in this Leader Guide may be used in multiple ways with a variety of groups who are traveling together on the journey to Christ. In addition to using it in adult Sunday school classes, consider the following ideas for study:

- **Sermon Series and Congregation-Wide Emphasis.** Many congregations have discovered the power of a congregation-wide focus with each household reading a chapter per week; sermons on each chapter on weekends; and discussion in all classes, Bible studies, Sunday school classes, etc., during a six-week period. Plan ahead with newsletter articles, website and e-mail announcements, a plan for distributing books to every household, and a calendar of sermon titles. (For more ideas, see *Focus on the Five Practices: A Congregation-Wide Initiative*, a set of resources based on the book *Five Practices of Fruitful Congregations*.)

- **Lenten Study.** *Five Practices of Fruitful Living* provides an excellent resource for spiritual preparation and learning during Lent for an existing class or study, a special Lenten study group, or for the entire congregation. Hold the orientation session and distribute books during the week before Lent and use the Leader Guide for a six-week series.

- **The Big Read.** Many communities, schools, and universities have discovered the power and helpfulness of selecting a single book and encouraging all members to read the book and all existing groups to discuss the book during a particular month or season. Congregations, districts, and conferences can hold "A Big Read" also. Publicize the emphasis repeatedly during a preparation phase, including information on how people can receive a book, and then remind members through e-mail, websites, and announcements throughout the reading period. Additionally, to spark more in-depth thought and inquiry, leaders may send focus points and discussion questions from the Leader Guide through e-mail or post to the church website.

- **Discipleship / Study Groups.** This resource is excellent for groups meeting on Wednesday evenings or another night of the week. Ensure members have access to copies of the book *Five Practices of Fruitful Living* in advance of the start of the study group, as well as group leaders, who need copies of both the book and the Leader Guide.

- **House / Cell Groups.** Some congregations initiate a number of gatherings in homes at various times of the week during a six-week period, inviting every member and attender of the church to participate short-term. Select leaders and hosts and offer a brief training for them using the Leader Guide. Develop a plan for inviting full participation, see that participants receive the book *Five Practices of Fruitful Living*, and assure hospitality in every home that hosts a group. The unifying effect of a congregation-wide learning experience can be powerful and transformative.

- **Family Discipleship Time at Home.** Encourage families/ couples to set aside time each week for a period of time to read and discuss the book and to pray for one another.

- **Extended In-Depth Study.** Focus on one practice per month.

- **Life Transition Groups.** Use with young adults, young married couples, new parents, parents of teens, empty nesters, retirees, divorce recovery, etc.

- **Exploration Through Journaling.** Form a small group that agrees to meet weekly. Using the Leader Guide outlines, break the chapters into shorter daily readings of 15–20 minutes followed by daily freestyle journaling for 30 minutes each day. Adapt the weekly gathering time to include sharing about what members have learned about themselves and their spiritual lives through their journaling.

- **VBS Study for Parents.** Offered while children are in Vacation Bible School, this works especially well for VBS programs held in the evening.

- **New Member Class, Discipleship Class, Exploring Faith Class.** *Five Practices of Fruitful Living* helps newcomers to the faith or to the church understand and explore the basic practices of Christian living.

- **Revival / Spiritual Renewal Emphasis.** This is an excellent resource for spiritual revival and renewal, whether in small groups or church-wide, as you learn to incorporate the five essential practices of fruitful, godly living into daily life.

- **Ecumenical Opportunity.** Invite other churches to participate, involve leadership from other area churches, and consider rotating meeting locations.

- **Community Outreach.** Advertise and invite people unrelated to your church to learn about the Five Practices of Fruitful Living. Hold the study sessions in a community center, library, or other community facility.

See www.fivepractices.cokesbury.com for additional resources and information.

APPENDIX E

Optional Activities for Longer Sessions/Retreats

The following activities are provided as extra ideas for longer group sessions or retreats. Feel free to modify the outlines and models in this Leader Guide as you wish to include these or other enrichment activities.

For example, for a 6- or 12-week study you might shorten your discussion or application time and choose one activity to do each week. Or for a weekend retreat, you might abbreviate the sessions on the Five Practices to 30 minutes each and follow each session with one of these activities. Be creative and make the study your own.

Radical Hospitality

Spend time "inviting God in" through meditation. Do a guided meditation activity or walk a labyrinth. (There are a variety of labyrinths, including floor labyrinths, finger labyrinths, and outdoor labyrinths.) Keep checking the Internet for more information and examples.

Passionate Worship

Work as a group to plan a short worship service with time for praise, prayer, and study/reflection. Create a time and space for a truly passionate worship experience in God's presence. If there are time constraints, plan the worship experience in advance.

Intentional Faith Development

Lead the group in *Lectio Divina* (spiritual or holy reading). This method of praying the Scriptures promotes communion with God and an increased knowledge of God's Word. There are numerous *Lectio Divina* exercises online.

Risk-Taking Mission and Service

Ahead of time, plan a service project to complete onsite or near your group session or retreat. Think outside your comfort zone. Or, take this time to plan a service project to do together in the coming weeks.

Extravagant Generosity

Instruct participants to keep track of their spending for one week prior to the group session/retreat and to bring their spending log with them. Discuss what this exercise revealed to them about their spending habits and priorities. Talk about what it would mean for them to live more simply and share practical ideas for reducing their spending.

Or, plan a special service of giving. Have participants reflect silently on how God is calling them to become more generous. Distribute index cards, envelopes, and pens and have them write their commitments on index cards and put them in a self-addressed envelope. Offer a prayer and have participants bring their envelopes to the altar. Collect the envelopes and mail them back to the participants at a designated time (3 months or 6 months later).

Offering God's Love

Brainstorm ways you might offer God's love in your community or the area where you are meeting. Or, do the brainstorming in advance and go and implement one of your ideas at the conclusion of the session/retreat. The possibilities are endless.

Notes

SESSION ONE
[1] Tillich quotes and references in Session 1 are from his sermon, "You Are Accepted," contained in Paul Tillich's *The Shaking of the Foundations* (Charles Scribner's Sons, 1948); pp. 161–162.

SESSION FOUR
[2] Frederick Buechner, *Wishful Thinking* (HarperSanFrancisco, 1993); p. 119.